NEW *and* SELECTED POEMS

1975–1995

NEW *and* SELECTED POEMS

1975–1995

THOMAS LUX

HOUGHTON MIFFLIN COMPANY

BOSTON   NEW YORK   1997

For information about permission to reproduce selections from this book,
write to Permissions, Houghton Mifflin Company, 215 Park Avenue South,
New York, New York 10003.

For information about this and other Houghton Mifflin trade and reference
books and multimedia products, visit The Bookstore at Houghton Mifflin
on the World Wide Web at http://www.hmco.com/trade/.

Library of Congress Cataloging-in-Publication Data
Lux, Thomas, date.
  [Poems. Selections]
  New and selected poems / Thomas Lux.
    p.   cm.
  ISBN 0-395-85832-1
  I. Title.
  PS3562.U87N4   1997
  811'.54 — dc21   97-430   CIP

Printed in the United States of America

QUM 10 9 8 7 6 5 4 3 2 1

The poems in *Sunday* first appeared in the following magazines: *Antaeus, Field, Footprint, Iowa Review, New Honolulu Review, Paris Review, Pequod, Ploughshares, Pocket Pal, Poetry, Quarry West, Quarterly West, Seneca Review, Virginia Quarterly Review.*

    The poems in *Half Promised Land* first appeared in *American Poetry Review, Atlantic Monthly, Crazy Horse, Field, Ironwood, Memphis State Review, Paris Review, Pequod, Ploughshares, Poetry, Rubicon, Seneca Review, Sonora Review.*

    The poems in *The Drowned River* first appeared in *Agni Review, American Poetry Review, Another Chicago Magazine, Antaeus, Boston Review, Columbia: A Magazine of Poetry and Prose, D., Denver Quarterly, Erato/The Harvard Book Review, Field, Iowa Review, Palmetto Review, Ploughshares, The Quarterly, Tray Full of Lab Mice Publications, Virginia Quarterly Review, Western Humanities Review, Willow Springs.*

    The poems in *Split Horizon* first appeared in *Achee, American Voice, Atlantic Monthly, American Poetry Review, Antaeus, Chronicle of Higher Education, Field, Greensboro Review, Gulf Coast, Harvard Review, Iowa Review, Midland Review, New Yorker, Passages North, Personal Crucifixion, Ploughshares, Phoebe, Seneca Review, Three Rivers, TriQuarterly, Virginia Quarterly Review, Volt.*

    The *New Poems* first appeared in *Alaska Quarterly Review, American Poetry Review, Atlantic Monthly, Chattahoochie Review, Iowa Review, Mudfish, New Yorker, Ploughshares, San Diego Reader, Sonora Review.*

    The author wishes to thank the National Endowment for the Arts (1976, 1981, 1988), the Guggenheim Foundation, and the MacDowell Colony.

Special thanks to Maria Elena Caballero-Robb, Raymond Clarke, Pamela Cohn, Stephen Dobyns, Ron Egatz, Jorie Graham, Mary Karr, Jean Kilbourne, April Lindner, Laura Nash, Michael Ryan, and Eve Wood.

— for my daughter Claudia
and for Rachel Colbert

. . . but in what is
ours, here, let
    justice be primary
when we sing,
    my dear.

    —HAYDEN CARRUTH

. . . to the most remote cell in the big toe.

    —SHERWIN B. NULAND

The general was busy with the ant farm
    in his head.

    —CHARLES SIMIC

CONTENTS

NEW POEMS

from SUNDAY 1979

from HALF PROMISED LAND 1986

NEW
POEMS

furnished rooms, flats, a hayloft,
a tent, motels, under a table,
under an overturned rowboat, a villa (briefly) but not,
as yet, a yurt. In these places
he has slept, eaten,
put his forehead to the windowglass,
looking out. He's in a stilt-house now,
the water passing beneath him half the day,
the other half it's mud. The tides
do this: they come, they go,
while he sleeps, eats, puts his forehead
to the windowglass.
He's moving soon: his trailer to a trailerpark,
or to the priory to live among penitents
but in his own cell,
with wheels. To take him, when it's time
to go, to: boathouse, houseboat
with a little motor, putt-putt,
to take him across the sea
or down the river
where at night, anchored by a sandbar
at the bend,
he will eat, sleep, and press his eyelids
to the window
of the pilothouse
until the anchor-hauling hour
when he'll embark again
toward his sanctuary, harborage, saltbox,
home.

REFRIGERATOR, 1957

More like a vault — you pull the handle out
and on the shelves: not a lot,
and what there is (a boiled potato
in a bag, a chicken carcass
under foil) looking dispirited,
drained, mugged. This is not
a place to go in hope or hunger.
But, just to the right of the middle
of the middle door shelf, on fire, a lit-from-within red,
heart red, sexual red, wet neon red,
shining red in their liquid, exotic,
aloof, slumming
in such company: a jar
of maraschino cherries. Three-quarters
full, fiery globes, like strippers
at a church social. Maraschino cherries, maraschino,
the only foreign word I knew. Not once
did I see these cherries employed: not
in a drink, nor on top
of a glob of ice cream,
or just pop one in your mouth. Not once.
The same jar there through an entire
childhood of dull dinners — bald meat,
pocked peas and, see above,
boiled potatoes. Maybe
they came over from the old country,
family heirlooms, or were status symbols
bought with a piece of the first paycheck
from a sweatshop,
which beat the pig farm in Bohemia,
handed down from my grandparents
to my parents
to be someday mine,
then my child's?

They were beautiful
and, if I never ate one,
it was because I knew it might be missed
or because I knew it would not be replaced
and because you do not eat
that which rips your heart with joy.

Or was it Princess Fall Winter Spring Summer?
Or Spring Summer Fall Winter?
I remember neither order nor the metrics.
I do remember she was slim,
her deerskin dress; she was good,
her heart. The puppet
had a wooden head,
checkered shirt, a painted grin,
and his jaw flapped up and down: open,
a black box, straight-lipped
dumb look when closed.
His cowboy suit and boots were wrong,
for a redhead
wearing freckles on his pinewood cheeks.
The show
sold shoes
between the things that made us laugh,
which I do not recall.
There was a cowboy: Bob.
There was a cranky old guy: Phineas T. . . .
Princess, where have you gone?
Princess, how fares our nation?
Princess, in the decades since
(once the decades hence)
how fare our nation's children
who once loved our nation's heart and face,
who once loved yours, Princess,
who once loved your heart and face?

CRISS CROSS APPLE SAUCE

— for Claudia

Criss cross apple sauce
do me a favor and get lost
while you're at it drop dead
then come back without a head
my daughter sings for me
when I ask her what she learned in school today
as we drive from her mother's house to mine.
She knows I like some things that rhyme.
She sings another she knows I like:
Trick or treat, trick or treat
give me something good to eat
if you don't I don't care
I'll put apples in your underwear. . . .
Apples in your underwear — I like that more
than Lautremont's umbrella
on the operating table, I say to her
and ask her if she sees the parallel.
She says no but she prefers the apples too.
Sitting on a bench
nothing to do
along come some boys — p.u., p.u., p.u.
my daughter sings,
my daughter with her buffalo-size heart,
my daughter brilliant and kind,
my daughter singing
as we drive from her mother's house to mine.

isn't very tall, 4 ft.
11½ inches, and can't speak
all day but waves a lot,
bobs to left and right, nods,
a little happy leap now
and then (his suit weighs 30 lbs.),
and a hundred snapshots a day
is the norm — a child or two or three enclosed
in his arms and paws. When asked
a question, as he often is, most often
about Uncle Owl,
his pal and the bigger star
in the cartoon from which the characters
are derived, he can't talk
but shrugs, hands out and open,
up to each side. He can't talk
because Chester Chipmunk
can't talk and he *is* Chester Chipmunk.
There are no small parts,
only small actors,
his high school drama teach said
and then said *That didn't come out*
the way I meant.
The man inside the chipmunk suit
wants to be inside the bunny suit,
or better, the monkey suit: there are sounds
to make, the part's a stretch.
His Method lessons have prepared him.
The man inside the chipmunk suit
has dreams just like you,
or her, or me, or them.
Above his sink is pinned
a picture of a minor movie star.

IMPINGEMENT SYNDROME

When one thing presses on another thing
and the result
is pain: could be in the shoulder,
elbow, knee, and the result is pain
and impaired movement.
It feels like pliers applied
to the bridge of your nose,
then wrenched. The result
is pain, in your body
or in your figurative heart.
Impingement: the bit-down jaws
of a gila monster (they won't let go),
a shark (they won't let go
until you're sawed in half).
Impingement: big toe
in the car door slammed,
the coffin lid you can't lift,
that which impedes movement
while causing pain
which impedes movement.
And to heal it
you push and pull over and over,
at this angle and that, against it.
You will not be frozen,
not your shoulder,
or neck, or knees, or heart,
you will not be frozen,
your range of movement made less, you will
whirl again your arms like a windmill,
your eye on the spot of pain
as it grows smaller: the entrance
to a cobra's burrow, then the eye of the spigot
that taps Satan's spine, until
it's the size of, and as deep as,
the final paragraph's last period's pinhead.

Only the Pope partook, the cardinals, priests, monks,
and nuns, it seems,
when you read the revisions. How the peasantry
reproduced itself despite
the bans is a mystery: no sex
on Thursday, the day of Christ's arrest,
Friday to honor His death,
Saturday in honor of His Mom,
Sunday, He has risen,
Mondays to honor all who have not risen . . .
It seems, given festivals and fasts
around Easter, Pentecost, Xmas,
that there were two to three days a year for sex if:
1) You did not enjoy it.
2) It was conceptual, heterosexual, man and wife, man
on top. Chronic
food shortages were made more bearable
by penitential fasting (bread
and water) for infractions: 7 days
for wet dreams, 20 days
for masturbation, 2 years
for interfemoral connection (penis
between thighs of passive partner). . . .
And despite inbreeding
as an offshoot of snobbery, the nobility
did not believe the priests either
which is why today there are so many sterile, dumb,
educated, and vacantly lovely humans
sitting in outdoor cafés
along the famous shopping boulevards.
Sex was sex: flesh
to flesh, eons of it, say one thing,
do another — fast, furtive,
fearful and God
was always watching,
with His big wide eyes,
watching what He had made.

A MAN TAKES HIS DAUGHTER, AGE FIVE, TO A PUBLIC EXECUTION BY GUILLOTINE, PARIS, 1857

He is a bad man. He says this in French,
to his daughter, in the same city,
in the same year Charles Baudelaire
published *The Flowers of Evil.*
The child's father believes
in this democratically applied machine,
painless, swift, humane: "A sweet maiden
whose embrace will waft one's soul
to heaven." "If you are bad . . . ," he says.
He read that Goethe had bought for his
son a toy guillotine
but this child could *see.*
He sits her on his shoulders.
I don't see the puppets, she says.
He is a bad man, her father says.
The crowd has seen all this before.
Some bring wine, food.
The blade gleams — it will be fifteen years
until it is painted black
to dim its glare,
a few more before rubber bumpers are added
to dull the double (the rebound) crash
of the blade.
Daddy, I still can't see the puppets.

and women with small heads
were everywhere
in my hometown when I was six.
Two men standing on the corner: small heads.
Small head: a woman leans to look in her mailbox.
Then there'd be some normal bodies, normal heads.
Not everyone,
in other words, in my hometown
had small heads
but many did, enough
that I'd say to my mother, father: *why*
does that man have a small head?
I was glad my parents'
heads were normal-size.
They were glad I (mostly) didn't ask
why a person with a small head
had a small head
within earshot of that person. Apparently
these small heads
did not appear so small to them.
They had my eyes checked first.
They took some x-rays of my skull.
Did I have migraines?
Did I have pinhead fears, dreams?
Perhaps it was the angle through the windshield glass?
The local Dr. leaning over me
with his penlight probing
my retina — his head was huge
and the hairs on the back of his hand
were crossed like swords. Nothing wrong
with my eyes or my brain
that he could tell
but the heads I swore were small
were not, they were just your average heads,
circa 1953,
just your average heads,
in America.

THE RIVER BETWEEN THE TRAIN
AND THE HIGHWAY

Branches bend to the river
as if to drink from it. The trees' roots
in the riverbank you'd think close enough
to have their fill
without this kneeling.
Is it some instinct the trees feel
to create circuit, a circular
current between the tree and the river?
Is it a drive
toward Oneness as the swami
from a desert country says?
I believe the trees, their branches,
are merely bent, beaten.
The banks are black, soaked by rain and oil
from the highway 30 yards above.
The trees are black and nearly bare.
The river, stream (what is the order
of diminishment: river, stream, brook,
rivulet, trickle?) is also black,
and shallow. It's going to join somebody
who's going to join somebody
who's going to sea. It won't
be back. It's going
to enter the sea
somewhere near a huge metropolis,
a beautiful and tortured city,
toward which the highway goes
and is terminus,
toward which the train goes
and is also terminus
in a house so large
it has its own sky and stars.

Mealy-bugs, shootflies in squadrons, mites.
A leech sucks your ankle.
A slug slides up your leg; curdled ooze, the glue
in the globs of it, leaky muck
and swampwater, a lacy scree
of green laid upon its surface, *glug,*
glug, mush and slough, bug manure.
Each step
each leg lugged
from its last footprint: you lean
back and pull a leg
from the sucking black
and haul it forward
and it becomes your front leg,
sinking. . . . Monkey scat,
snake scat, rat scat, fish.
Blackwater, blackwater, runnels of oil,
the marrow, the pith
of grasses, of reeds, of spines: foetid
and fangs and fear — but, *and,* too, *as well as*
the breathing and heat
of a billion writhing
and alive things,
a food chain, cell chain, (little) heart chain
from microbe to Yahweh,
from quicksand to elevator,
from the greased pneumatic tube to hell
to the placid glacial lake.
The mud hums with its mud-loving beetles,
and their cousins once removed,
the waterpenny beetles,
moored in their riffles,
the waterpenny beetles
love where they live.

THE VOICE YOU HEAR
WHEN YOU READ SILENTLY

is not silent, it is a speaking-
out-loud voice in your head: it is *spoken,*
a voice is *saying* it
as you read. It's the writer's words,
of course, in a literary sense
his or her *voice,* but the sound
of that voice is the sound of your voice.
Not the sound your friends know
or the sound of a tape played back
but your voice
caught in the dark cathedral
of your skull, your voice heard
by an internal ear informed by internal abstracts
and what you know by feeling,
having felt. It is your voice
saying, for example, the word barn
that the writer wrote
but the barn you say
is a barn you know or knew. The voice
in your head, speaking as you read,
never says anything neutrally — some people
hated the barn they knew,
some people love the barn they know
so you hear the word loaded
and a sensory constellation
is lit: horse-gnawed stalls,
hayloft, black heat tape wrapping
a water pipe, a slippery
spilled chirr of oats from a split sack,
the bony, filthy haunches of cows. . . .
And barn is only a noun — no verb
or subject has entered into the sentence yet!
The voice you hear when you read to yourself
is the clearest voice: you speak it
speaking to you.

WHAT MONTEZUMA FED CORTÉS
AND HIS MEN

Tamales, they like tamales,
new to them (corn), dipped in honey,
or with pimiento
served on black or red earthenware plates,
cocoa with honey
in painted gourds: they were gods, this
was breakfast, 10 A.M. Lunch
was early afternoon, the hottest time — Montezuma
and his more numerous boys (in the many
thousands) ate corncakes, beans, tomatoes
but Cortés and his 500
got that plus
venison, dog, turkey, lots of turkey, pheasant,
partridge, boar, iguana, water fowl
from Lake Texcoco.
They were also offered
but did not like — they were gods! — thistles, rats
with sauce, newts, waterfly
larvae, tadpoles, ants, agave worms.
They did like: egg of salamander (an eely
European taste) and pats of lake scum (tasted
like Manchegan cheese).
There is no mention in the chronicles
that peyote or mushrooms were offered,
perhaps because Montezuma and his priests
ate them all
which would help
explain why they thought Cortés was a god.
After lunch everyone — even later
when the fighting began — took a nap.
Dinner was late — 9, 10, 11, it was cooler
and the food more or less like lunch.
No need to tell you about arrows and stones,
harquebuses and swords.
Or the horses.
No need to tell you about the room full of gold.

These were gods
and they were hungry, always hungry,
and it had been prophesied that they were coming,
sailing in from the east
on the backs of big water birds,
sailing to an old world they called new,
on a clear sunny day
in the spring of 1519.

TORN SHADES

How, in the first place, did
they get torn — pulled down hard
too many times: to hide a blow,
or sex, or a man
in stained pajamas? The tear blade-shaped,
serrated, in tatters. And once,
in a house flatside to a gas station,
as snow fell at a speed and angle you could lean on,
two small hands (a patch of throat, a whip
of hair across her face)
two small hands
parting a torn shade
to welcome a wedge of gray light into that room.

TOWARDS

— for Rachel

Towards you
on wheels — car, bus, cycle, truck, scooter, (roller)
skates, trolley, tram, tumbrel.
Towards you
like every river on the Andes' eastern slopes
towards the Amazon: unceasing, around, or pooling
for a while then spilling downhill
again; through, as in how a tunnel
is drilled through a mountain. Towards you
by air: jet, turbo, prop, balsa biplane driven
by a *big* rubberband, jumbo
airbus, on Dumbo's
neck, one-seater copter,
homing (you are home) pigeon's pouch — hyperbole,
perhaps; rhapso-babble,
but true. In a car
towards you: how many yards,
therefore seconds, lost
changing lanes, two more red lights
instead of green?
Towards you more oxygen
each breath, towards you
each mile lifts lead x-ray vests
from my chest, each mile
grievy needles
removed from my eyes.
Towards you I'll take a sled, chariot (swing low),
rent a llama. I'll run
two miles, walk one,
run two towards you, towards you
I am on a sure course,
every inch of sail aloft,
towards you: harbor, origin, heart.

COMMERCIAL LEECH FARMING TODAY

— for Robert Sacherman

Although it never rivaled wheat, soybean,
cattle and so on farming
there was a living
in leeches
and after a period of decline
there is again
a living to be made
from this endeavor: they're used to reduce
the blood in tissues
after plastic surgery — eyelifts, tucks,
wrinkle erad, or in certain
microsurgeries — reattaching a finger, penis.
I love the capitalist
spirit. As in most businesses
the technology has improved: instead
of driving an elderly horse
into a leech pond, letting him die
by exsanguination,
and hauling him out
to pick the bloated blossoms
from his hide, it's now done at Biopharm
(the showcase operation in Swansea,
Wales) — temp control, tanks, aerator
pumps, several species,
each for a specific job. Once, 19th century,
they were applied to the temple
as a treatment for mental
illness. Today we know
their exact chemistry: hirudin,
a blood thinner in their saliva,
also an anesthesia
and dilators for the wound area.
Don't you love
the image: the Dr. lays a leech along
the tiny stitches of an eyelift.
Where they go after their work is done

I don't know
but I've heard no complaints
from Animal Rights
so perhaps they're retired
to a lake or adopted
as pets, maybe the best looking
kept to breed. I don't know. I like the story,
I like the going backwards
to ignorance
to come forward to vanity. I like
the small role they can play
in beauty
or the reattachment of a part,
I like the story because it's true.

You could put an X here.
You could draw a picture of a horse.
You could write a tract,
manifesto — but keep it short.
You could wail, whine,
rail or polysyllable celebrate.
You could fill this space
with one syllable: praise.
The only requirement,
the anti-poet said,
is to improve upon the blank page,
which, if you are not made blind
by ego, is a hard task.
You could write some numbers here.
You could write your name, and dates.
You could leave a thumbprint,
or paint your lips and kiss the page.
A hard task — the blank
so creamy, a cold
and perfect snowfield upon which
a human, it's only human,
wants to leave
his inky black and awkward marks.

like a downhill brakes-burned freight train
full of pig iron ingots, full of lead
life-size statues of Richard Nixon,
like an avalanche of smoke and black fog
lashed by bent pins, the broken-off tips
of switchblade knives, the dust of dried offal,
remorseless, it comes, faster when you turn your back,
faster when you turn to face it,
like a fine rain, then colder showers,
then downpour to razor sleet, then egg-size hail,
fist-size, then jagged
laser, shrapnel hail
thudding and tearing like footsteps
of drunk gods or fathers; it comes
polite, loutish, assured, suave,
breathing through its mouth
(which is a hole eaten by a cave),
it comes like an elephant annoyed,
like a black mamba terrified, it slides
down the valley, grease on grease,
like fire eating birds' nests,
like fire melting the fuzz
off a baby's skull, still it comes: mute
and gorging, never
to cease, insatiable, gorging
and mute.

A SMALL TIN PARROT PIN

Next to the tiny bladeless windmill
of a salt shaker
on the black tablecloth
is my small tin parrot pin,
bought from a bin,
75 cents, cheap, not pure tin — an alloy,
some plastic toy tin?
The actual pin, the pin that pins the pin,
will fall off soon
and thus the parrot,
if I wear it, which I will,
on my lapel. I'll look down
and it'll be gone.
Let it be found by a child,
or someone sad, eyes
on the sidewalk, or what a prize
it would be for a pack rat's nest.
My parrot's paint
is vivid: his head's red, bright yellow of breast
and belly, a strip of green,
then purple, a soft
creamy purple, then bright — you know
the color — parrot green
wing feathers. Tomorrow I think
I'll wear it on my blue coat.
Tonight, someone whom I love
sleeps in the next room,
the room next to the room with the black tablecloth,
the salt shaker, the parrot pin.
She was very sleepy
and less impressed than I
with my parrot
with whom, with which I
am very pleased.

from

SUNDAY

1979

SOLO NATIVE

Suppose you're a solo native here
on one planet rolling, the lily
of the pad and valley.

You're alone and you know
a few things: the stars are pinholes,
slits in the hangman's mask.
And the crabs walk sideways
as they were taught by the waves.

You're the one thing upright
on hind legs, an imaginer,
an interested transient.
Look — all the solunar tables
set with silver linen!

This is where you'll live, exactly
here in a hut on the green and gray belly
of the veldt. You'll be

a metaphor, a meatpacker,
a tree dropping or gaining
its credentials. You'll be

a dancer with two feet dancing
in the dirt-colored dirt. All this,
and after a few chiliads,

from your throat a noise,
an awkward first audible
called language.

THE GREEN

I don't know why the moth
on the other side of the window
beating the poor dust off his wings
I don't understand why
he wants to get in here. If

he did get in he'd have no visual
diversion but himself in the mirror —
which is all I have — and which is a boring
diversion. Meanwhile,

the clouds, between the earth
and the moonlight, are lame
and beg to be dispersed. I know the forest,
in the darkness, is still green

and I believe when it is nearly dawn
a sparrow will land on the chair
on my porch. The lower half
of her beak will be missing,
she can't eat,
and she is still alive.

RILKE AND LOU

Rainer must go.
— Lou Andreas-Salomé, from her journal

Of course, Lou noticed the angels
in Rilke's pockets and hat
but wondered: Does he have to be a poet
all of the time? That,
actually, wasn't the real problem.
Rainer was a sweetheart,
too sweet, hanging
around too much. Besides,
he practically wept every time
a leaf fell from a tree.
Jesus! thought Lou, this guy
will devour me, or try
at least — he's rather frail — so
let's unload him, fast.
Only because she had bigger genius,
you understand, than any poet,
any philosopher — Nietzsche's
a good example — and was certainly up there
in insights with Freud.
And, as we come to expect
from all illuminati,
she was angry
when she saw the other angels,
angry at the end
that they were coming.

THE BITTERNESS OF CHILDREN

Foreseeing typographical errors
on their gravestones, the children
from infancy — are bitter.
Little clairvoyants, blond, in terror.

Foreseeing the black and yellow
room behind the eyelids, the children
are bitter — from infancy.
The blue egg of thirst: say hello.

Foreseeing the lower lips of glaciers
sliding toward their own lips, the children
from infancy — are bitter.
Them, rats, snakes: the chased and chasers.

Foreseeing a dust-filled matchbox, the heart,
the temples' temples closing, the children
are bitter — from infancy.
From the marrow in the marrow: the start.

BARN FIRE

It starts, somehow, in the hot damp
and soon the lit bales
throb in the hayloft. The tails

of mice quake in the dust,
the bins of grain, the mangers stuffed
with clover, the barrels of oats
shivering individually in their pale

husks — animate and inanimate: they know
with the first whiff in the dark.
And we knew, or should have: that day
the calendar refused its nail

on the wall and the crab apples hurling
themselves to the ground. . . . Only moments
and the flames like a blue fist curl

all around the black. There is some
small blaring from the calves and the cows'
nostrils flare only once
more, or twice, above the dead dry

metal troughs. . . . No more fat tongues worrying
the salt licks, no more heady smells
of deep green from silos rising now

like huge twin chimneys above all this.
With the lofts full there is no stopping
nor even getting close: it will rage

until dawn and beyond, — and the horses,
because they know they are safe there,
the horses run back into the barn.

DAWN WALK AND PRAYER

I step out onto the porch a few minutes
short of dawn

and hear the deaf
and nearly blind
old woman next door coughing.

Since this is the hour of exhaustion
and insomnia I'll walk for a while
on the beach since it's here

in front of me now as it usually
isn't. I love the light

at this hour — I call it dim
disappearing. I also love the boats:
flipped over, their hulls
turned to the sky. They're facts

of this world I would kiss
or at least caress: things that belong
underwater turned and touching

their opposite: air.
At this hour I could get away

with a kiss or a caress.
But I won't try — I'm thinking
about my neighbor. To be deaf

and practically blind
and now also with a cough:
That's why I'm making this prayer.

It's still the same, Charles.
Every day dislimned, the heart clicking
erratically — the sound of amateurs
playing billiards. How are you enjoying
the high privileges of the dead?
The double
triple and more turns
of the dark, the delicious
please of quietude? No one,
no thing is different: the oblati swarm,
the poor are formed into lines
leading poorer. . . . There's one good thing,
Charles: the few beautiful verses
granted you by God
sing. Even though you're deaf
I want you to know
they sing! You should know that,
Charles, it's still the same.

All the slaves within me
are tired or nearly dead.
They won't work for money,
not for a slice of bread.

Tired or nearly dead,
half underwater, wanting
merely a slice of bread:
the inner slaves, singing.

Half underwater, wanting
only a few flippers to swim,
the inner slaves, singing
the depth-charges within.

Only a few flippers to swim!
And a sensor to sense the sound
of the depth charges within —
that's all they ask for aloud.

A sensor to sense the sound,
a hearer to hear the small aurals:
that's all they ask for aloud.
They're slaves with slaves' morals.

Hearers hearing small aurals,
they won't work for money.
They're slaves with slaves' morals,
all these slaves within me.

I wonder if they sleep better here
so close to the elemental pentameter
of the sea which comes in incessantly?
Just a few square acres of sand
studded mainly with thick posts
as if the coffins beneath were boats
tied fast to prevent further drift.
I half stumble around one pre-dawn,
just a dog following the footprints
of another dog with me, and stop

before one particular grave: a cross
inlaid with large splinters of mirror.
Whoever lies here is distinguished,
certainly, but I wonder — why mirrors?
For signaling? Who? No, they're embedded
in the stone and so can't be flicked
to reflect the sun or moonlight.
Is the sleeper here unusually vain
and the glass set for those times of dark
ascensions — to smooth the death gown,

to apply a little lipstick to the white
worms of the lips? No again. I think
they're for me and the ones who come
like me, at this hour, in this half-light.
The ones who come half-drunk, half-wild
and wholly in fear — so we may gaze
into the ghosts of our own faces,
and be touched by this chill of all
chills, — and then go home, alive,
to sleep the sleep of the awake.

ELEGY FOR FRANK STANFORD

1949-1978

A message from a secretary tells me first
the heavy clock you were
in your mother's lap
has stopped. Later, I learn who
stopped it: you,
with three lead thuds,
determined insults, to your heart.
You dumb fuck, Frank.
I assume, that night, the seminarians
were mostly on their knees
and on their dinner plates only a few
wing bones — quiet flutes
ahead of the wind. . . . I can almost
understand, Frank: your nerves'
oddometer needle waving
in *danger,* your whole
body, in fact, ping-raked, a rainbow
disassembling. You woke, in the dark,
dreaming a necklace of bloodsuckers. . . .
But that final gesture,
Frank: irreversible cliché!
The long doorman of the east continues
his daily job, bending slightly
at the waist to wave dawn past.
Then the sparrows begin
their standard tunes, every day, Frank,
every day. There's the good hammer-
music in the poles
of north and south; there's the important
rasp of snake over desert and rock;
there's agriculture — even when it fails:
needle-sized carrots, blue pumpkins;
and presidencies, like yours, Frank,
of dredging companies, but presidencies. . . .

You must have been desiring exit badly.
So now, you're a bit of gold to pound
back into the earth, the dew, of course,
forever lapping your toes, —
Frank, you dumb fuck, — who loves you
loves you regardless.

I want you, spider: walker-on-the-ceiling,
creeping black thumb.
Here's my forehead, the pad
for your landing. So slip
down your rope, that purest advance
of saliva, settle close
enough to my lips.

I'll know what you know,
thank you. Exhort, tell the story
of the eight-leggers. Put your fur
next to mine, relax down here
on the pillow. You look like a priest
in a multisleeved cassock
so let's confess

to each other: We're beasts,
twelve limbs between us,
sharing one house, the same desires
and industry: to design
the web, live on what we catch
from air, and always returning,
always, to the spun eluctable cave.

PORTRAIT OF THE MAN WHO DROWNED
WEARING HIS BEST SUIT AND SHOES

When his small skiff returned alone,
like a horse who's lost its rider,
the relatives sat down on stones

by the shore and waited for the tide
to bring him, also. He had wanted
to row back, singular and drunk,

from a wedding on a neighbor island,
just a few real miles away
across the black calm. The relatives

waited, the tide did
what it does, and he arrived
in that familiar pose

of all the drowned: face down, chin
tucked in, arms outstretched
with slightly cocked wrists,

and legs a bit splayed — the position
of a man trying to fly somewhere,
somehow. The Dead Man's Float

it's called by the living
which carried him home on a flight
both airless and lacking a wing. . . .

Hand over hand and over the backs
of some humans it comes

as it does now, from the south, south-
east. It comes, beginning nowhere

and hauling all the expelled
breaths of millions, from nowhere,

a foot or a thousand feet above
the oceans, carrying and not

caring. It comes — an enormous zero
that encircles whatever objects

it whirls around. It's this wind
that touches me here and maybe

again some endless miles north,
or west, or . . . In the back

of my eye it's always there
dividing whatever leaf from whatever

tree — dull, unrelenting, dumb.
And also its sour taste rattling

across my tongue. . . . O immortal
and awful marriage between velvet

between velvet pliers and a velvet
noose: the wind, the enemy.

GOLD ON MULE

On his knees with that pickaxe,
the sluice, the pan — all for a palm
full of dust. Valuable
eventually. Right now, the sun slams
on the wing of a fly
seeking moisture around the eye

of a mule waiting for his back
to be piled with gold. Poor bastard,
first he walks up here with sacks
of flour, beans, and sooner or later
leaves downhill, heavier, loaded.
It gets turned into money.

It's a sweat to get this stuff
and it's ugly from the rock.
The secret of minerals must be polish,
all the swipes of vanity applied
to what is really dirt. Rare
dirt, sure, but dirt on the spines

of mules — balanced like gold.
The man keeps digging, hacking out
a vein for what he needs: who
can name it? There's a slow shout,
nobody hears, in the air.
The man digs. The mule stares.

Force-feeding swans — let me tell
you — was hard. And up
every morning 4:30 counting

the lambs out to pasture,
each one tapped on the forehead with a stick
to be sure it's there.

Uncle Reaper half the time so drunk
he'd pull his milkstool
under the horse: more work

explaining the difference. Gramma
and Cousin Shroud putting up
8000 jars of beets, Auntie Bones

rapping her wooden spoon
against my ear: "More bushels, bumbler!"

I'll tell you — I understand
how come the dancing bear tore off his skirt
and headed back to the Yukon,
how come all of a sudden jewels in avalanche
down the spine of my sleep. . . .

But still, still when it rains
I remember all of us: farmers, simple sweatmongers
of the dirt whose turnips depend on it,
I remember how we called it down, how down
we desired it to fall: the rain.

POEM IN THANKS

Lord Whoever, thank you for this air
I'm about to in- and exhale, this hutch
in the woods, the wood for fire,
the light — both lamp and the natural stuff
off leaf-back, fern, and wing.
For the piano, the shovel
for ashes, the moth-gnawed
blankets, the stone-cold water
stone-cold: thank you.
Thank you, Lord, coming for
to carry me here — where I'll gnash
it out, Lord, where I'll calm
and work, Lord, thank you
for the goddamn birds singing!

Here's to Samuel Greenberg
who died of bum lungs, age 23,
in 1916, penniless,
leaving only a few notebooks
as a gift to Hart Crane
who died of bum lungs (i.e., filled
with seawater), age 33, in 1932.
Here's to you, Samuel — semi-illiterate
coughing it out among total
illiterates during the only time
in your life you had time
to write: on your back,
on a cot, on Wards Island
preparing nearly inaudible gifts
of language, which were used,
as collaboration, in a few lines,
in a few poems by Hart
Crane — who had a little
more time to sing through his mouth.
Here's to you, Samuel Greenberg,
small master, and here's to your bones
which glow and are sliding
beneath the earth, with the earth. . . .

VIEW FROM A PORCH

Thud, thud, all the sores go blind,
and over the basket of pears hover
brief addicted fruitflies.

The bruises on the pears are also blind.
The barn is blue — as far
from the Mediterranean as possible.

You'd think the residents serious here — each one
scattered lonely as a cow-pie — you'd think:
blood-in-the-rafters. . . . But if you listen,

both ears, close, you'll hear a plow parting
earth; closer, some worms unburied
nervous. The chirpers are happy,

the humans go about jobs — in barn,
field, or house — healing,
unhealing, and sky again

is admitted to the dumb-lovely dirt
turned over and over, turning
its worn yawn wide:
breathing, nearly alert.

MAN ASLEEP IN A CHILD'S BED

— for Crystal Reiss, who loaned me hers

Here's a man who falls hard asleep,
who sinks beneath the rim of air humming
a dim song, a threnody.
With him is a drowsy animal, his tongue,
and also the inner curtains of the mirror.
Only one thing visible: a small oh of breath.

Above the sleeper: one circle called breath.
A wedding ring of oxygen above a mouth asleep
and the long backward glance of the mirror.
There's a particular tune to his humming,
the tone is familiar, the tongue
comfortable, and the threnody

nearly light, a light threnody
of the lungs being lungs, the breath
riding back and forth over the tongue.
Here's a man fallen hard asleep.
Now here's the sleep-chortle, the humming
man behind the two-way mirror

of a dream, of a dream of a mirror
black on both sides. His threnody
is deep now, not quieter, his humming
deeper. He takes a breath, another breath,
innumerables. . . . He's far asleep,
and asleep in his mouth: his tongue.

Resting, it's an ancient tongue,
the one every man presses to the mirror,
every woman presses, while asleep,
to the glass, the faint threnody
which is a repetition of certain breath.
This is a surviving sleeper, humming

a constant tune, a raw humming,
quiet down to the root of the tongue.
Quiet like the gone breath
of the dead who moved and left a mirror,
who left, who left a threnody.
He is asleep and with them, asleep.

He's humming now, deep, the mirror
draws in its tongue, the threnody
is breath, and the dreamer's body, asleep.

The horses out of their brains bored all
winter gnawing on stalls
Outside the snow several fetlocks deep
Pounding our noses
against the ice everywhere
you could say
we had our souls in backward
we were dumb from trudging away from noon
we were lame like the bread that lies on the table
One child's dream sledding down a slag heap
every day going at it with the cold

* * *

So he deposits the moth in a matchbox
and flails with a flashlight
into the forest a mile or two fox-
like crosses a few gullies streams
stopping finally beyond a final ravine
where he slides open removes the moth
lays down the light on the perfect
theater of moss
as backdrop a few slim branches
and on that greenly illuminated stage it dances
to an audience of darkness plus one

* * *

He was absolved prematurely they forgot
what he might do from the point
of absolution to the next point what's it called
So he filled in he could do anything
He disregarded the live hearts
of live humans he did misconduct before
his mother and father he coveted
his neighbor's wife and speedboat
he propped open a baby's eyes with matches
He did it like a good thief
having already been absolved

* * *

The mattress always acts as a raft
He's aware of that that's why he hopes
to bob in the wakes there
He never takes a path nonchalantly solo
knowing that's of course where
beasts do their dreaming also
He joins nothing He joins the other peasants
waving pitchforks not getting
dung for our wheat we've had it
up to our haircuts thinking we're salved
until we're mistaken is obvious

        * * *

Approximately dawn some people exercise Take X
He goes out to a dirt road
with a club and bashes small stones
like in a ballgame Sending
a shot deep into the east slows down dawn
The first peeps of light In India
they have a word for it it's a child's name
you can't make a close paraphrase
The very beginning light
when roof and bush and animal
become apart from air

        * * *

As if hands were undoing our clothes from the inside
we fumble around in a rowboat
One oar floats downriver What a day
On the opposite shore Mallarmé's
feeding some swans How will we row
Which port our oars arriving
days ahead of us With you
voyaging you also voyaging
There's the lovely sword of moon
There's the cricket warming up his cello
There's the various positions in which we exult

        * * *

Once gone like gloss in a flashflood
Once an animal loving another of another species
Once one joyful crumb of the fully individual
Once a convict dreaming of mowing a hayfield
Once an avenue upon a bench sits one moment of present
Once under deep enough to ring the literal sleep-bells
Once the dead changing shirts in their small booths
Once farmers merely bored by drought
Once all the birds invented as toys
Once the heart-angles the trillion u-turns of blood
Once the flying noise

* * *

Slow tarantula slow blink by blink
the afternoon unspools a wind primping
the fir tree's common hair
A blue calf bleats in the far pasture
Reduced by bucolia
it always hauls him back
gaping like a lump of gold shocked
in the sludge-sifter's hand
One water moccasin rolls over a few times
A hill hunches somewhat
while memorizing the earth's sore fictions

* * *

His mouth connecting lines the puzzle
from nape to the slope beneath
her ankles the dunes He takes
pleasure there and giving it it's simply the hearts
simply the lungs simply two
to swerve beneath the fell cleavers of day to day
Their nerves on overdrive together
two odd ones warbling around an oasis
alert to the blue thuds in the wrist
And that other pulse the pulse of top lip
to bottom lip and bottom lip to top

* * *

Loving the incunabula the beginnings
like one obsessed by desert
loving its freeze at night
because it reminds him more of water
than the heat of afternoon Lined
up and loaded like something on wheels
small wafers of anger off his bureau
spinning A window is open
On the table there is sky
And behind the curtain one marvelous belly
or else the wind is bringing the usual

from

HALF
PROMISED
LAND

1986

THE MILKMAN AND HIS SON

— for my father

For a year he'd collect
the milk bottles — those cracked, chipped,
or with the label's blue
scene of a farm

fading. In winter
they'd load the boxes on a sled
and drag them to the dump

which was lovely then: a white sheet
drawn up, like a joke, over
the face of a sleeper.
As they lob the bottles in

the son begs a trick
and the milkman obliges: tossing
one bottle in a high arc,
he shatters it in midair

with another. One thousand astonished
splints of glass
falling. . . . Again
and again, and damned
if that milkman,
that easy slinger
on the dump's edge (as the drifted
junk tips its hats

of snow), damned if he didn't
hit almost half! Not bad.
Along with gentleness,

and the sane bewilderment
of understanding nothing cruel,
it was a thing he did best.

55

"There was poverty before money."

There was debtors' prison before inmates,
there was hunger prefossil,

there was pain before a nervous system
to convey it to the brain, there existed

poverty before intelligence, or accountants,
before narration; there was bankruptcy aswirl

in nowhere, it was palpable
where nothing was palpable, there was repossession

in the gasses forming so many billion . . . ;
there was poverty — it had a tongue — in cooling

ash, in marl, and coming loam,
thirst in the few strands of hay slipping

between a pitchfork's wide tines,
in the reptile and the first birds,

poverty aloof and no mystery like God
its maker; there was surely want

in one steamed and sagging onion,
there was poverty in the shard of bread

sopped in the final drop of gravy
you snatched from your brother's mouth.

You've seen them, these semi-urban birds
who live, not in, but on the edge of great cities.
No longer wild — of the cornfield, or resting high
in rafters of deserted tobacco barns. They venture
to the borders, but will not cross, where city sends
its last tendrils out and park gives edge
to woods, where the first lawns
larger than billiard tables grow
each block a little larger
with the houses. These crows

like old and gnarly pines
to graze beneath, aloof, and to sit in. They are not
so bold as smart and seem to know that laws exist
against the discharge of shotguns upon them.
Old blue-black aristocrats, they prefer
to saunter, at midday, across lawns
of pine nuts abundant, the best spots
to steal what lesser birds hold dear.
Maybe this is why a group of them is murder.
They are everywhere where they never used to be.

I hate to see it: a bird so crafty, so sure,
moving in where it's easier to eat
and they grow dim. What logic
sends them here and not so far away
only fieldhands know them? Maybe
they come to us, to live among us
so they can claim it as *their* choice —
which makes them proud and bright,
though does not cease their doom,
nor preserve their haughty, haunting cry.

I suppose that we were shocked
but doubt the reading level dropped
among the members of the Blue Jays
(those between the Eagles and the Crows)
when one of us shot his mother and didn't show
up at school. It's safe to say he wasn't missed.
We didn't like him (he held my head
between a door and the jamb and pressed)
but this was something else: shot her dead.

Bobby the lonely
Bobby the mad
shot the only mother he ever had
Shot her and shot her
until she was dead
Like a screen door slamming
the neighbors said

Maybe this is how the habit of metaphor begins.
Maybe it starts with terror up to our chins.
He went away to "a home" until he was old
enough to go to court, and thence to jail.
It would surprise me if he got any mail.
No father was around so the house was sold;
I remember the sign — everybody pointed it out.
It was November, the police done, and it was cold.
Nobody forgave him, especially the brutes and the louts.

Bobby the lonely
Bobby the sad
shot the only mother he ever had
Shot her and shot her
until she was dead
Like a screen door slamming and slamming
the neighbors said

How parched, how marrow-dust dry
they must get on their long surface and undersea
journeys — huge stuffed husks,
imperturbable swimmers grazing
jellyfish abutting the bruised
waters' pasture. How thirsty
a sixty-day swim, how graceful
the winching back to one unforgotten
shore. *Plub, plub,* sleepless
the hull's inner workings, their tails
motorless rudderings; deep,
deep their thirst and need. One hundred,
one hundred and twenty: how long they live
in their thirst, propelling
the great bloody steaks of their bodies,
dreaming, anticipating alert,
single-purposed oblivions: sweet
sweet turtle-sex — which excites
the lonely watches of sailors — sometimes days
joined in wave-riding rapture on the surface
of the depths. And still more thirsty
afterward, how alone later (currents
having taken) — righted, relentless,
back on course, collision, with centuries,
with a shore: solitary, speechless,
utterly buoyant, as unethereal
as cabbage. How thirsty these
both wise and clumsy, like us, feeding
in ever-widening or diminishing circles,
outward and inward, dropping
great oily tears, killing themselves
to beat a big hole in dirt,
burying something, then retreating
heavily on their own tracks, like rails,
reaching forward to the sea.

SOMEBODY'S AUNT OUT SWABBING
HER BIRDBATH

Somebody's aunt out swabbing her birdbath
with Lysol and the town papermill down the block
is beginning to blister in a clean shock
of light. You drive away. The math

is grammarschool: x thousand workers,
y hundred jobs. The shoe factory closed last year.
Nobody's starving, but the church is in fear
it'll lose some customers.

A man steps out into his backyard's yellow air —
apart from his mortgage, his gripes.
He is perfectly lighted by secret animal stripes.
As you drive away a blunt wind parts his hair.

GIVE IT TO THE WIND

If the wind touches your cheek
in a manner that pleases you,
then to it give something back.
Give some dollars, a good slice
of bread, a phrase from a woman
who loves you; open an ampule
of joy and wave it, out loud.
If you find a dime, then give two
to a beggar, celebrate

nerve endings, your soup.
If whole minutes exist
when to your left is a river with ducks
and to your right a cathedral slashed
by light, then carry clean bandages
to a battlefront, swab foreheads
in a contagious ward; if a few
cells bloom, a synapse heals,
then stab a thousand tiny flags

into the graves of generals,
then mourn a murderer's childhood.
And if, after furious sleep,
the room is windy
and cool air slides across the blank
dunes of your sheet, then thank
the night for the day
and the day for what
it is: liable to be.

For some semitropical reason
when the rains fall
relentlessly they fall

into swimming pools, these otherwise
bright and scary
arachnids. They can swim
a little, but not for long

and they can't climb the ladder out.
They usually drown — but
if you want their favor,
if you believe there is justice,
a reward for not loving

the death of ugly
and even dangerous (the eel, hog snake,
rats) creatures, if

you believe these things, then
you would leave a lifebuoy
or two in your swimming pool at night.

And in the morning
you would haul ashore
the huddled, hairy survivors

and escort them
back to the bush, and know,
be assured that at least these saved,
as individuals, would not turn up

again someday
in your hat, drawer,
or the tangled underworld

of your socks, and that even —
when your belief in justice
merges with your belief in dreams —
they may tell the others

in a sign language
four times as subtle
and complicated as man's

that you are good,
that you love them,
that you would save them again.

Early on, this decade's light smelled
like something burning and now
of something smoldering, the end
of the decade smells: the grave, forever
lingering of limb-smell exploded, some
bodies, many, of our generation blown
every which way, gone. And choking
on that smell we created another: the faint,
exhausted, perfumed puffs of ennui. A whole
generation looking over its shoulder
retromancing nothing, using the peripheral
(nothing), and forward? The future.
It's arrived — forgetfulness, jobs,
even some money, which we didn't want,
but which we got, our actual share,
actually. To purchase amnesia
it doesn't take much. — We could count
the dead and they would be mostly
men, and then we could count the women,
mostly alive, whose turn it is now,
nailing down each day with an *X*
of something done on a calendar
creeping toward a new century.

1979

His job is honest and simple: keeping
the forest tidy. He replaces,
after repairing, the nests
on their branches, he points every pine needle north,
polishes the owl's stained perch,
feather-dusts the entrance
to the weasel's burrow, soft-brushes
each chipmunk (the chinchilla
of the forest banal), buffs antlers, gives
sympathy to ragweed, tries to convince —
like a paternal and inept psychiatrist —
the lowly garter snake to think
of himself, as he parts the grass,
as an actor parting the stage curtain
to wild applause, arranges, in the clearing,
the great beams of light. . . . This is his job: a day's,
a week's, a life's calm, continuous,
low-paying devotion. At dawn
he makes a few sandwiches and goes
to work. *I love this,* he thinks as he passes
the wild watercress — its green as stunning
as surviving a plane crash — in the small,
inaccessible swamp.

It's the little towns I like,
with their little mills making ratchets
and stanchions, elastic web,
spindles, you
name it. I like them in New England,
America, particularly — providing
bad jobs good enough to live on, to live in
families even: kindergarten,
church suppers, beach umbrellas. . . . The towns
are real, so fragile in their loneliness
a flood could come along
(and floods have) and cut them in two,
in half. There is no mayor,
the town council's not prepared
for this, three of the four policemen
are stranded on their roofs . . . and it doesn't stop
raining. The mountain
is so thick with water, parts of it just slide
down on the heifers — soggy, suicidal —
in the pastures below. It rains, it rains
in these towns and, because
there's no other way, your father gets in a rowboat
so he can go to work.

At the far end of a long wharf
a deaf child, while fishing, hauls in
a large eel and — not
because it is ugly — she bashes its brains
out of eeldom on the hot
planks — *whamp, whamp, whamp,* a sound
she does not hear. It's the distance
and the heat that abstracts
the image for me. She also does not hear,
nor do I, the splash the eel makes
when she tosses it in her bucket,
nor do we hear the new bait
pierced by the clean hook, nor
its lowering into the water again.
Nobody could. I watch her
all afternoon until, catching nothing
else, she walks the wharf toward
me, her cousin, thinking
with a thousand fingers. Pointing
at our boat she tells me
to drag it to the water. She wants me to row
her out to the deep lanes of fish.
Poetry is a menial task.

THE NIGHT SO BRIGHT A
SQUIRREL READS

The night so bright a squirrel reads
a novel on his branch
without clicking on his lamp.
You know you're in a forest — the stars,
the moon blaring
off the white birch. . . . You could walk
out with your wife
into the forest, toward the fields beyond,
you could walk apart from her,
and still see her. It's so bright
you need not talk nor fear
that particular sticky abrasion you get
by walking into pine trees. You find
a lucidity in this darkness.
Your wife is here — three or four
trees away — you recognize her profile,
and you do not think she is anyone else,
here with you, a hundred
or so yards now from a field where,
in an hour or so, you might see
dawn's first deer browsing, or an owl,
soaring home after the shift he loves,
a fat sack of field mice under his wing.

You go to school to learn to
read and add, to someday
make some money. It — money — makes
sense: you need
a better tractor, an addition
to the gameroom, you prefer
to buy your beancurd by the barrel.
There's no other way to get the goods
you need. Besides, it keeps people busy
working — for it.
It's sensible and, therefore, you go
to school to learn (and the teacher,
having learned, gets paid to teach you) how
to get it. Fine. But:
you're taught away from poetry
or, say, dancing (*That's nice, dear,
but there's no dough in it*). No poem
ever bought a hamburger, or not too many. It's true,
and so, every morning — it's still dark! —
you see them, the children, like angels
being marched off to execution,
or banks. Their bodies luminous
in headlights. Going to school.

If I die before I wake
I pray the Lord my soul to take. . . .
From a common enough
and nondenominational child's prayer.
Not too unlike a lullaby, it's a simple
pledge in verse before hitting
the dark night after night
and one line ringing
a few times in the mind: *If I die*
before I wake. Oh, the generations
of insomniacs created,
the night-light industry booming!
But let's face it: prayer is good,
particularly for children.
They should understand some things
so they might appreciate
them. Like: the buzzards and the bees,
what those stone visors mean,
poking up, on lawns behind fences,
in rows, whitish dominoes. . . .
They should know: it's a sleepy journey
to a half promised land
and you never wake at all.

There were some summers
like this: The blue barn steaming,
some cowbirds dozing with their heads
on each other's shoulders, the electric fences
humming low in the mid-August heat. . . .
So calm the slow sweat existing
in half-fictive memory: a boy
wandering from house, to hayloft, to coop,
past a dump where a saddle rots
on a sawhorse, through the still forest
of a cornfield, to a pasture talking to himself
or the bored, baleful Holsteins nodding
beneath the round shade of catalpa, the boy
walking his trail toward the brook
in a deep but mediocre gully,
through skunk cabbage and popweed,
down sandbanks (a descending
quarter-acre Sahara), the boy wandering,
thinking nothing, thinking: Sweatbox,
sweatbox, the boy on his way
toward a minnow whose slight beard
tells the subtleties of the current, holding there,
in water cold enough to break your ankles.

His spine curved just enough
to suggest a youth spent amidst a boring
landscape: brokedown corncrib, abandoned sty,
skeletal manure shed, a two-silo barn with one
sold off leaving a round pit
filled with rubble — where once the sweet silage
piled up and up now the brooding
ground of toads. And then the barn
began to buckle like an ancient mule falling
first to one knee, then both,
rear haunches still bravely, barely aloft.
Whatever hay left huddling in corners
more fossil than vegetable.
This landscape exists — in many
places — and is almost lovely,
even in, even in spite of, its decay.
It endures in histories
and in fiction: the crabapple, the gray
pastures, the dried dung
how many years old? — And atop the barn
a weather vane knocked askew by a rifle shot,
pointing straight up, as if all the winds
were going to heaven.

MOON-ANNOYED, COGNAC'S
ASHEN THRILL

Moon-annoyed, cognac's ashen thrill
diminishing, irritated by sunlight,
decent sleep, good food, and piles
of money — nothing helps
the heebie-jeebies when they start, like hunger
revving up, when they begin their tossing cruise
beneath the skin, hauling the spine
erect with fear. Nothing. Nothing
helps. What are the origins (embryo,
embryo, where are you going,
what do you know)? Nobody can say,
or will, but it's got to do,
you can bet, with death, which,
some people will tell you, is a part
of life. Right. Personally,
I don't care. It's over you others
I worry, why you worry. How can you fear
what hardly equals the blank wash
of rain on slate shingles,
how can you fear what is not sleep,
what is not quiet, what is sexless,
what has no memory, what lacks
imagination, what does not . . . ?

It must be the monk in me,
or the teenage girl. That's why I'm always off
somewhere in my mind with something
stupid (like a monk) or spiritual
(like a teenage girl). Sometimes, there's vision,
by reason of faith, in glimpses, or else,
and more often, a lovely blank, a hunger
like Moses' hunger when with his fingernails
he scraped the boulders of their meager lichen
and then fiercely sucking them. . . . It's a way
of living on the earth — to be away
from it part of the time. They say
it begins in childhood: your dog
gets runned over, your father
puts a knife to your mother's throat. . . .
But those things only make you crazy
and don't account for scanning,
or actually mapping, a galaxy inside. I believe
it happens *before* birth, and has to do,
naturally, with Mom. Not with what she eats,
or does, or even thinks — but with what she *doesn't*
think, or want to: the knot of you growing larger
and, therefore, growing away.

AFTER A FEW WHIFFS OF
ANOTHER WORLD

After a few whiffs of another world
he decided to stay with the stench
of the present: dumpster lids everywhere
rising like cakes, garbage scows
moving in long orderly lines
across the harbor. . . . The olfactory — he loves it
even when it wafts, wracking all points
of the compass. It's always invisible
and takes its direction according to the whimsy
of wind, or fans, or the waves
of a hand. Cave dwellers knew it,
and dogs. The bare smell
of dirt on cabbage, the snow-
on-your-arm smell. Even
in the abstract: fear-smell, like spit
on a knife blade. And
what the worms inhale, and then
the smell of dew on barbed wire, the sweet,
thick smell of sex, slick,
our lungs giddy and pink with it. . . .
It's not the world which is good or bad
and so we run our noses over everything.
Even the dumb have this sense.

THE DARK COMES ON IN BLOCKS,
IN CUBES

The dark comes on in blocks, in cubes,
in cubics of black measured
perfectly, perfectly
filled. It's subtle and it's not,
depending on your point of view.
You can measure it best in a forest,
or in a grassy lowland, or in any place
where your lamp is the only lamp and you can turn it off.
To describe it the usual adjectives
of the gray/black genre will not do. It's not light,
nor is it the absence of light, but
oh, it's sweet, sweet like ink
dropped in sugar, necessary and invisible
like drafts of oxygen. Absolutely,
in squares, in its containers of space,
the darkness arrives — as daily
as bread, as sad as a haymow
going over and over a stubble field,
as routine as guards
climbing to gun towers
along penitentiary walls, clicking
on their searchlights
against it.

LIKE A WIDE ANVIL FROM THE MOON
THE LIGHT

Like a wide anvil from the moon the light
on the cold radiator and all the windows in a row
along the spine close — zeros winding tight.
And to make the rattlesnakes feel at home?
A private cactus farm. There's not an eek's chance
of getting out of here. Some apples, bruised,
mute, are nailed back to their branches,
and the south wind — low, hot ash — cruises
through a crook in the apple tree's trunk.
The dirt, not known for its tenderness, on its knees
somewhat, and one munificent ant carries a crumb
to the crumbless. Every pond on earth agrees:
they are tired of being dragged — all those hooks —
for drowned children. All this beneath
the ceaseless lineage of comets! Books
help a little: groan-soaked, one broken etc. thief,
tree surgeons lost above tree lines,
chasmed sidewalks, a hatful of blanks,
sore-got ore. . . . Yes! — it does, it does feel exactly fine
crawling ashore, emptying the boots of water, and frankly
here's to the clouds the color of bone,
here's to the indecipherable path home,
here's to the worm's sweat in the loam. . . .

BENEATH THE APPLE BRANCHES
BENT DUMBLY

Beneath the apple branches bent dumbly
with the blank weight of their blossoms —
the grass and me — completely
alive with one thought
like a shin struck with an axe: What
is the same each summer? I know
that the ring of cold slung
through my chest grows colder, that the mountains'
lowly crags grow imperceptibly rounder, but what
is the same? Not the driveway
littered (in a few months) with crushed
apples swarmed by yellowjackets — those cruel
insects, not the hackneyed
rock garden, its pool for goldfish
long filled in with dirt and a few
ill-bred petunias, not the heat bugs
and their high whine. . . . What
is the *same?* Only the incomparable chins
of horses, only a desire
to place the mural of a pond
horizontal as it belongs,
only the long haul in the linear world, ongoing.

The Oxymoron sisters, Snowflake and Acetylene,
returned from Camp Hatchet today, pale
and furious, loaded down with camp-
crafted ashtrays and pillowslips,
the sweetlings. You should love them
both: the shy Snowflake,
with her albums and albums
of pressed fern (at age seven,
the family story goes, she petitioned
to change her name to Fern), her neck
like cream, holding in its curve the hope
of a second world, a world aswarm
with passivity, one lacy,
yawn-laden afternoon after another,
wind chimes sonorously lighted . . . *serene*
Snow distant Flake. And then
our Acetylene: taller, nervous, her tack-
hammer fists tattering the air as she talks.
Acetylene the acute, the keen,
in her memory some long blades
hardened by fire. Acetylene — arrested
for arson in kindergarten, pet prank
of filling ice trays with lighter fluid.
They're home from camp today, again
among us and around us, our darlings,
our fearsome sisters inside
and out; these precious, necessary,
these two — both of whom,
despite nominal redemptions,
no matter how much we love them,
both of whom are ugly
and dying.

Dr. Goebbels did not go to heaven. The mundane,
and worse — murderous — literature
of his soul will not come down to us;
not even among the lesser ranks
will this dramatist come down to us
as sometimes the most obscure can do, giving
some sense of what it is,
this walk around on earth. Dr. Goebbels's
novels, plays, and poems
will not be read — not even for insights,
historical, into his character.
His theories about language
were simple: *its best use is for lies.*
This was no monster,
nor was the thing he believed in,
which was nothing. Dr. Goebbels
did not go to heaven, as he wished,
with his wife and six poisoned
babies (4½ to 14!). This was no monster,
being too vain, having no ideas,
and hating the sight of blood.
He showed the world one limit of language
(written or spoken — but always
written first): it can give us
what we need to keep on hating.
Dr. Goebbels did not go to heaven,
nor did he burn in hell.
It was in the chancellery
garden where he burned — an ordinary man,
in ordinary petrol — in fire so hot
that on his bad foot
it warped the brace.

THE SWIMMING POOL

All around the apt. swimming pool
the boys stare at the girls
and the girls look everywhere but the opposite
or down or up. It is
as it was a thousand years ago: the fat
boy has it hardest, he
takes the sneers,
prefers the winter so he can wear
his heavy pants and sweater.
Today, he's here with the others.
Better they are cruel to him in his presence
than out. Of the five here now (three boys,
two girls) one is fat, three cruel,
and one, a girl, wavers to the side,
all the world tearing at her.
As yet she has no breasts
(her friend does) and were it not
for the forlorn fat boy whom she joins
in taunting, she could not bear her terror,
which is the terror
of being him. Does it make her happy
that she has no need, right now, of ingratiation,
of acting fool to salve
her loneliness? She doesn't seem
so happy. She is like
the lower middle class, that fatal group
handed crumbs so they can drop a few
down lower, to the poor, so they won't kill
the rich. All around
the apt. swimming pool
there is what's everywhere: forsakenness
and fear, a disdain for those beneath us
rather than a rage
against the ones above: the exploiters,
the oblivious and unabashedly cruel.

My friends, I hope you will not swim here:
this lake isn't named for what it lacks.
This is *not* just another vacant scare.
They're in there — knotted, cruel, and thick

with poison, some of them. Others bite
you just for fun — they love that curve
along the white soft side of your foot,
or your lower calf, or to pierce the nerves

with their needles behind your knees.
Just born, the babies bite you all the same.
They don't care how big you are — *please*
do not swim here. There is no shame

in avoiding what will kill you: cool pleasure
of this water. Do not even dip your toes
in because they'll hurt you, or worse,
carry you away on their backs — no,

not in homage, but to bite you as you sink.
Do not, my friends, swim here: I like you
living: this is what I believe, what I think.
Do not swim here — lest the many turn to few.

WIFE HITS MOOSE

Sometime around dusk moose lifts
his heavy, primordial jaw, dripping, from pondwater
and, without psychic struggle,
decides the day, for him, is done: time
to go somewhere else. Meanwhile, wife
drives one of those roads that cut straight north,
a highway dividing the forests

not yet fat enough for the paper companies.
this time of year full dark falls
about eight o'clock — pineforest and blacktop
blend. Moose reaches road, fails
to look both ways, steps
deliberately, ponderously. . . . Wife
hits moose, hard,

at a slight angle (brakes slammed, car
spinning) and moose rolls over hood, antlers —
as if diamond-tipped — scratch windshield, car
damaged: rib-of-moose imprint
on fender, hoof shatters headlight.
annoyed moose lands on feet and walks away.
Wife is shaken, unhurt, amazed.

— Does moose believe in a Supreme Intelligence?
Speaker does not know.
— Does wife believe in a Supreme Intelligence?
Speaker assumes as much: spiritual intimacies
being between the spirit and the human.
— Does speaker believe in a Supreme Intelligence?
Yes. Thank You.

Tottering and elastic, middle name of Groan,
ramfeezled after a hard night
at the corpse-polishing plant, slope-
shouldered, a half loaf
of bread, even his hair tired, famished,
fingering the diminished beans
in his pocket — you meet him.
On a thousand street corners you meet him,
emerging from the subway, emerging
from your own chest — this sight's shrill,
metallic vapors pass into you.
His fear is of being broken,
of becoming too dexterous in stripping
the last few shoelaces of meat
from a chicken's carcass, of being moved by nothing
short of the Fall of Rome, of being stooped
in the cranium over some loss he's forgotten
the anniversary of. . . . You meet him,
know his defeat, though proper
and inevitable, is not yours, although yours also
is proper and inevitable: so many defeats
queer and insignificant (as illustration:
the first time you lay awake all night
waiting for dawn — and were disappointed), so many
no-hope exhaustions hidden,
their gaze dully glazed inward. — And yet we all
fix our binoculars on the horizon's hazy fear-heaps
and cruise toward them, fat sails
forward. . . . You meet him on the corners,
in bus stations, on the blind avenues
leading neither in
nor out of hell, you meet him
and with him you walk.

TRIPTYCH, MIDDLE PANEL BURNING

It happened that my uncle liked to take my hand in his
and with the other seize
the electric cow fence: a little rural
humor, don't get me wrong

no way child abuse. He
took the voltage first
and besides it only slaps and never burns,
or even seems to bother

the cows. It's merely a small snake
flying up your arm (it feels most
peculiar at the first wrist), across
your shoulders (there's a slight

buzzing, though, still in your top
vertebra), and down
the other until it — the shock — explodes
at the end of each of your five free

fingertips. Thank you, Uncle.
You made sure I'd never murder — not
after they fried the guys who deserved it
in the movies. Society, and I, thank you.

You also kept me from the mental hospitals
when that was all in fashion — for fear
of the electrodes to my temples. And thus,
you saved me and my insurance carriers

some money so we could buy more goods,
which is good for all of us. Thanks. I count
it as a normal childhood, so prosaic
the traumas — say, a live, for several hours,

Japanese beetle wedged beneath a cast
on a broken arm — that only once did I fully believe
in God: when He clearly punished me
for a stupid and embarrassing act

of cruelty. I liked it fine alone
amidst the asunder of a purely American loneliness:
a decline of conscience simultaneously
with the instinctual conscience of a child's

trying to form. It was 1955
and America was as arrogant as it ever gets;
we'd polished off a few wars, a lot
of our fathers were gone for good

and we were ready for what matters: lucra-
tive employ, bomb shelters, a few scoots
in the bank, babies, a fat Sunday
dinner. Art didn't matter much, so what,

nor generosity. We, as a nation, earned
our ignorance and the right to pass it on.
— These memories are so banal and so sweet
they almost *attack* me: How I survived

a pitchfork tossed at my chest, how I survived
(with more difficulty) algebra's x's and y's,
how the hayfields hid me, how the perfume-bottle-cleaved
smell of a fresh-plowed field or a field

after first thin snowfall spread
with hot manure made me feel *perfectly*
alive. Even what died
did not bother me — I understood

that simple reality. When I came across
the severed head (a neat powder-burned
pencil-sized hole between its wide eyes) and legs,
and entrails, and tail of a cow I'd fed

through a spring, summer, and winter,
I understood. I knew where stew meat
and flank steak came from, and though
I liked that Angus I was pleased

to see that, in fact, they *do* have three stomachs.
Her face, I admit, looked surprised — not
bloody and so neatly severed — and I tested
its heaviness to see if I could carry it,

under my arm, to school. I even understood
and appreciated the meatflies' swarm
and ecstasy. I poked the bellies
with a stick — they were blue — and figured

it was time to smoke the cigar I'd filched
somewhere. As I said, it was a normal
childhood, but still I was astounded
by ignorance — my own — and by what I guessed

was missing. What America stressed was: engineers
we need; money happy, and otherwise it don't matter
so long as you don't cause trouble. Once
I saw the near-idiot neighbor boy rape

a chicken, killing it, and judging
by the noise, causing it great pain as well.
He never felt so smart and I could tell
he liked being in charge, knowing what, for once,

he was doing. Later, he told his father
it was the fox come again and could he kill it
too? His father sadly and savagely beat him
with a rake. I thought I could teach

this boy to read — until he set the books on fire.
It was never that I ever thought: what
am I doing here, me, one of the sensitives;
it was more: this is exactly where I *do*

belong, this is it as it truly exists.
And when I would stare into the coals
after a family barbecue the dull orange glow
seemed to me as beautiful as color

ever gets. The midsummer evening chill
would descend on my arms and not once
did I ever fear death, or life. Hay smell
was everywhere, Lord Jesus, we had the third-best

water in these United States, two wars over,
my sweet father still intact,
my mother strong and never
oppressed, and yet I knew something was wrong
as well as I knew something was right.

2

Is true that you get born dumb and bald as a ball-
peen hammer and as bald
and dumb you expire. So it's. In between,
you choose to live in a manner you can live with,
you build what you can build, and you learn,
as Mr. Stevens says, you learn to reject
the trash. And down it goes here: the rage
and ugly of that trash, the noisome,
the suppuration and putrid: *that which will not
do.* Like a bad black piece of cheese you want to give back

all the lies and crooked imaginings — as green,
loose, and valuable as duck drops, all the sad
homilies, like noses with a thousand pustules, pustules
on top of pustules (like folding campcups),
the knitting needles plunged into your ear
to quiet the mind's terrible machine,
the singular obsessions endlessly revised: the design
of a mummy case, all that business
about the Sandman, how he puts you to sleep
(Who wouldn't under dunes of it?)
and then coins like sandbags piled up
against false flood: you have to pass it *back*
to your fathers, your slaves, to your baby bonnets
deranged — so that the bad half
of an idiot savant you won't be: you have to pass it back,
not on: all the fat and artless, all
creation unable to escape a niggardly self,
all the art of brilliant solipsism, all scrofulous
associations with *fine* wine or haute couture
and the attendant doilylike sophistications,
the exclusives beating the poor to death
with crystal fingerbowls, spearing
them with diamond stickpins: the humiliation

of poverty: you must
give it back — no man or woman should feel
it — like a hypodermic needle broken off
at skin level, and then another and another
until there's a beard of them, a *physical*
humiliation: no one should be forced
to bake bread with scraps and burnt matches:
nothing like *odium dei* do I call for,
only some way to say to each other: a higher
power controls me and I invented it to be gentler
than yours — my power gentler than yours!: I say
what I reject most is adamant self-love
and self-justification — in all their costumes,
those cruel constructions of suet: I spit
on the lapel of a pompous man because he robs
another of self and himself of dignity, I spit
on the lugubrious surveyors of personal internal
disaster areas calling for federal help,
the self-hagiographers, those who crush
the blooming milt's possibilities in the same way
every (every!) kindergarten — vessel for shame — child
in America is told and told again to imagine
that imagination is something to be dispensed
with: I'm rattling with rage over what I simply
want to reject: not only the wearing
of your victim's toes and ears around your neck
but also the position you have to put him in
to take them, not only dread but also its rancid
chopping block with blood pounded
into its grain, not only the cruelty
of inarticulated love, or sex, but also selfishness
of tongues, not only colossal indifference
but also its cause, not only shark attacks but also
their really rubber teeth: I won't
accept it anymore, I reject

it: the cruelty of aggression and the cruelty
of withdrawal, love with hard bark
on it, a grueling insistence of form,
loverboy, greasy mongrels of the groin — let me
be not distant, nor man nor woman from me,
let me not need to write palinode after palinode,
let me take rage and divide it
again and again until is left one grain upon my palm
to blow away — cruelty and stupidity — and soon
I shall crawl out of a great pit, soon
I will crawl its slimy walls
out, fierce toeholds holding, little helpful
hooks my fingernails — it's got to be rejected:
blueprints too blue, architects building barracks
for peasants to live in
while they build mansions for generals, the peasants'
gruel and its lumps accepted *as course,*
the beautiful verses filled
with vermin, the sad devotion of flagellants,
the stupefacients fed us daily,
the quotidian humiliations and the rare
humiliations, all that which causes
the terrors, the bloody taciturnity, all
the blink-blown, irrevocable severings. . . .

If there are, each day, terrors
we have to live with
let them be: that we fail to *make*
something (*anything,* in whatever
realm: a new lilypad,
a way to line one extra belly
with nutrients, a tool
to scan and receive the vision of God);
and, of course, of course: that we not
be able to love.

3

It's clear: a future, there should be
a future. Once he was (he was!) drawn to,
devotedly, the recondites of death,
another side. He thought it absorbing
and only didn't like that he could go there one-way

only. It was a thrill to hit 100 m.p.h., slam
his eyes, and count off seconds: 3, 4, 5,
while standing harder on the pedal — a kind
of sad, athletic exercise. No longer
does he indulge in that. In fact, he'd like back

those doltish days wasted
in pursuit of erasure. But there's no fruit
in that longing: blanks gone
are gone, the seeds in the doom rattle
settle — silent, level. What shivers

of loathing that remain are bell-beacons clanging
happily above a reef's razors. It's enough
that he's waived the hard slide
down a frozen chute. There's no need to hurry
it — oblivion — since for us it comes

on its own time: passive, patient, neverminding
our white and bloody knees.
He won't listen to poems anymore
about the other shore and its sweetnesses
(their original points that he missed?)

nor does he care about the obvious or bland
alternatives: Oh, a little house, power,
a piece of land. He wants to own nothing
but his heartbone banging, born of anything.
He doesn't want a little wife, he wants a big

wife and he wants their babies
dancing with Daddy alert as an eland,
dancing with Daddy divested of fear,
dancing with Daddy lucidly, lucidly, clear.
Of the past he can't change one hair,

the future he can't invent and will be wary
even in dreaming it.
It's like this: a speaker
has the moment in which he speaks — and that
is a raging, bloom-sodden abundance: a dilated sky

crammed with air (but its outer-
zoned, infinity-harking edges eaten
by Zyklon B, rads, megatons . . .) wholly
breathable, the heart and lungs perpetual
machines ready to run, eyelids lifting

like birds off cool water. . . . One can choose
to live on this orb or die
on it: between the two
he's no longer shredded. — In a papery pinnace,
a twine-bound flyboat, he circled

a teetering globe: a long winter chewing
his shoes at Port Famine, several months tapping
his cane around *Isla Desolación,* a hundred
heated nights huddling through dead
calms. The best burning ground he leased,

piled the kindling chin-high (powdered with resin,
soaked in pitch), tortured and confessed,
and invited a crowd to his own at-the-stake;
his own buboes, blisters he abetted,
and blains. Quenchless, he stood

berating no one (a flat pan of warm-
as-bathwater bay before him), berating what he could see
of the moon, the night.
Pure peroration, his head shaved
and with a bull's-eye painted

on his bitten skull. If there was an answer
he could not hear it.
Supercilious, blind and writhing
like a maggot in a hogshead of filet mignon,
he said: Bring it down, loose your toothiest landslide,

Lord, I want it, I'll take all the aches
you have, give it to me open-bore
and wide-pattern — so I can go. . . . But
for whatever reasons his pieces
were not snatched up by Whosoever's talons

and dropped on rocks washed pale
by bird dust. For whatever reason was offered,
and he took: manumission, a sliver
at first, then a wider crack, then wider
into which he wedged a bony hip, and then more

open, like an *O*, a circle, not
a zero, and there was one whiff
of sweet air. It was not a paradise
he got a glimpse of, it was of *this*
world, an incessant reality, a multi-edged

wholeness. And it will do. It will do.
It was not for lack of trying he did not die.
Wavering, the patient suddenly
took a turn toward better, the crinkling
oxygen tent filled with blue light

(in a bearded God he doesn't believe,
nor in the crows who serve him) — there was just
a little light: electrical, metaphysical,
mizzling on a thousand pinpoints;
no symbol like an *X* burned his forehead,

there was a coin of light; no voice inside
or further inside, not one choirboy did appear;
it was only a light made up of particles of light,
it was just a black table soaked
in light and then the black broke down,

split apart, dispersed with a purpose — like drops
of blood borne off a battlefield
on the backs of ants, and following: rain, rain.

from

THE
DROWNED
RIVER

1990

BACKYARD SWINGSET

Splayed, swayback, cheap pipe
playground: a swing, a slide, some rings
maybe — we love our babies,
and a tire hanging from a branch
won't do. For one summer
it shines — red, the chains of silver,
and beside it the blue plastic pool.
First winter out it goes to rust.
I love America's backyards,
seen from highways, or when
you're lost and looking

hard at houses, numbers.
The above, plus a washed-out willow,
starveling hedge, tool shed
a dozen times dented,
and a greasy streak
against the garage where a barbecue
went berserk. A Chevy engine block
never hauled away
or the classic Olds on chocks. . . .
Beneath the blue-gray humps of snow: pieces
of a summer, a past

Mom said to pick up,
but they weren't.
Now, nobody's home, all across America
nobody's home now.
Brother or sister is, in fact, on Guam,
or working nightshift at the box factory,
or one is married and at this moment
wiping milk rings from a kitchen table.
And Mom, Mom is gone,
and the ash on Father's cigarette grows so long
it begins to chasm and bend.

Bend your back to it, sir: for it will snow all night.
How gently they sink — white spiders,
multi-bladed bleak things,
these first, into the near mirror
of your shovel's surface. It snows,
lightly — wide columns
of black between each flake —

but it will snow all night, and thicker.
So you start now and scrape
your driveway of its first half inch.
Every hour you will plow
it down and up again.
It's not a grave
you dig, nor a path to school,

nor is there a dot of philosophy
in this work: you clear it as it falls
so as not to lift the heavy load at dawn.
The lanes behind you whiten,
imperceptibly hiss, and several —
smoke-roses, epaulets — bite
your back, your closed shoulders.

So soft, stubborn, it falls, parting
the streetlamp's light
harder, larger, and the whole cold neighborhood
bandaged. On the corner
the salt and sand box,
the mailbox (such white
on blue!) could be art

but aren't. You should move
a little faster now behind
the shovel — push once your twenty feet
of drive and it fills.
Soon it will take two.
Bend your back to it, sir: for it
will snow all night.

CELLAR STAIRS

It's rickety down to the dark.
Old skates, long-bladed, hang by leather laces
on your left and want to slash your throat,
but they can't, they can't, being only skates.
On a shelf above, tools: shears,
three-pronged weed hacker, ice pick,
poison — rats and bugs — and on the landing,
halfway down, a keg of roofing nails
you don't want to fall face first into,

no, you don't. To your right,
a fuse box with its side-switch — a slot machine,
on a good day, or the one the warden pulls,
on a bad. Against the wall,
on nearly every stair, one boot, no two
together, no pair, as if the dead
went off, short-legged or long, to where they go,
which is down these steps,
at the bottom of which is a swollen,

humming, huge white freezer
big enough for many bodies —
of children, at least. And this
is where you're sent each night
for the frozen bag of beans
or peas or broccoli
that lies beside the slab
of meat you'll eat for dinner,
each countless childhood meal your last.

ELEGY FOR ROBERT WINNER

1930–1986

I dreamed my friend got up and walked;
he was taller than me
and we were young, striding
down some stairs, two at a time, headlong,
on our way to sports or girls.
What did it mean — my psyche
freeing him, freeing me? My friend
is gone; no, no metaphors: dead, who broke
his neck in 1946, six months
before I was born, and then forty years

in a wheelchair. A medical
miracle — he's in the textbooks — to live that long
with a shattered spine,
and now he's dead, whom I loved.
He was a poet and administered
a cemetery — a profession, a business
like any other. He had an office there,
and now a grave.
Mostly we talked poetry, not business.
In my dream I wished we'd smashed his chair,

sent its bent wheels wobbling
over a cliff; or I wished we'd run
to where the boulder is — just beneath
the surface of the stream — on which
he broke his neck,
and dove in together, emerged,
dove again, and emerged. . . .
I dreamed my friend got up and walked.
We were striding down some stairs
and he was tall, taller than me.

No matter what you do
you cannot hold it long
or take it back again.

The sky, the barely blue
blank sky, the tight moss-bound
houses of sleep, will call.

No matter how hard you love,
that love will pass, will pass,
your friends imparadised,

gone, lost. The summers blaze,
the years, and what you know
grows dim, hurt by the dark.

No matter child, or wife,
or art. The river bends
and bends again seaward.

The soft lip-click of worms,
a spider's feet across
a leaf: you see, you hear.

No matter blessings, rage,
or rest: the dead stay dead.
You walk, spine alive, you kneel,

you lay your ear down on
the ground. Does God live there?
Does God live anywhere?

SO YOU PUT THE DOG TO SLEEP

> I have no dog, but it must be
> Somewhere there's one belongs to me.
> — *John Kendrick Bangs*

You love your dog and carve his steaks
(marbled, tender, aged) in the shape of hearts.
You let him on your lap at will

and call him by a lover's name: *Liebchen,*
pooch-o-mine, lamby, honey-tart,
and you fill your voice with tenderness, woo.

He loves you too, that's his only job,
it's how he pays his room and board.
Behind his devotion, though, his dopey looks,

might be a beast who wants your house,
your wife; who in fact loathes you, his lord.
His jaws snapping while asleep means dreams

of eating your face: nose, lips, eyebrows, ears . . .
But soon your dog gets old, his legs
go bad, he's nearly blind, you puree his meat

and feed him with a spoon. It's hard to say
who hates whom the most. He will not beg.
So you put the dog to sleep. Bad dog.

You get sent to the workhouse because you worked
and worked
yourself so deep in debt
you took a loan to pay the debt,
then another to pay the interest on the loan
(all the while working: day labor,
night labor, and thumping
a bowl of porridge on the table each noon
for the kids and wife) and then
you make a deal with the local loanshark
who's happy to help you out
but breaks your knees the following week
when the bank won't remortgage your house
so you can pay his vig. Times
are hard. So like I said, you get sent to the workhouse
where you don't work (no jobs
there and everybody else ditto
out of work) and your only visitors
are creditors demanding
that you pay them. Then you die
and they put your body in the deadhouse
at the workhouse — which is like stabbing
a stab wound — until your wife or son
comes in with some money
to buy a box and buy you out of the deadhouse
through the workhouse
and hauls you home
and next goes out to borrow some money
to buy some dirt
into which they sink your box.

TRAVELING EXHIBIT OF
TORTURE INSTRUMENTS

What man has done to woman and man
and the tools he built to do it with
is pure genius in its pain. A chair of nails
would not do without a headrest of spikes
and wrist straps pierced with pins.
The Head Crusher, for example — "Experts disagree
about this piece: is it 17th or 18th century?"
This historical hatband contracts and contracts,
by screw, and was wrought by hand.
These skills, this craft, get passed along.
Take *The Red Hot Pincers and Tongs.*
They were "addressed mostly to noses, fingers, toes.
Tubular pincers, like the splendid crocodile
shown here, served to rip off . . ." I have been in pain
at museums, openings, but not
like this: *The Heretic's Fork* — "Placed
as it is, allows the victim only to murmur: I recant."
In all the pictures
the men and women chosen do not
appear in pain: sawed lengthwise,
wrecked on a rack or wheel, they do not
look in pain. And the torturers
(the business always official)
seem uninterested, often flipping
pages of a book — one of laws, of God.
It seems most times men did this or that,
so terrible to him or her,
it was because God willed it so.
Or, at least, they thought He did.

The skeletons covered with sores — if they can walk,
this is where they're sent; whoever's civic pulse
is uncertain, thready; he whose only thought's
a picture: *el vomito negro*. The half-wits,
the borderline nincompoops, left-handed pinheads;
collectors of rats' feet; the boy who torched
his grandmother's cat, the grandmother
who torched her granddaughter's doll — you'll find them

here: on Green Ward, Hilarity Section, Sedation Floor.
Those permanently broken
in spirit, who won't pray
or denounce prayer, who admire Jesus personally
but never mind the Immaculate etc. —
they're all sent here. The surfeit-sensitives,
the metromaniacal, sociopathetics,
the non-numb psychically hyper, loaded

in vans, pried from the streets
with spatulas, snatched at recess from playgrounds,
from circles of jeering peers, hauled
from factories and offices — they're all
here. The boy who collected
15,035 lbs. of snake
pounded those not already flat flat
and stacked them in his room. The girl

this moment in Morbid Ward for pinching
the hearts of canaries, or the teenager,
on her way to hard-water hydrotherapy,
who would not believe
her boyfriend or the president:
they're all here — in paper slippers,
no pants — brought for study,
for adjustment, help, removal, cure.

KWASHIORKOR; MARASMUS

An unknown river whose banks drip feathers,
orchid petals, wherein live fish
mysterious; a medieval scholar, humanist
scamp. No, a rare, rich dish, thick

with crème fraîche; the local junior high
known for annual bake sales.
A beautiful African princess, two
thousand cows her dowry; a town

in New Jersey. A defunct balm
or salve; a tree whose boat-shaped leaves
are prized for love potions. A long-forgotten,
one-sided battle won easily by imperialists;

a ship lost rounding the Horn,
not a single spar or beam washed ashore.
A name but no face
from a dream; a rich uncle

kids are named after in hopes of . . .
An Arab pastry; a lower prophet,
saint of bad luck and the empty beggar's bowl.
Two more words, by heart, to learn.

It's a cold cold piece of meat,
this cadaver's heart, this black gash
of a river between white banks.
Cold to its center, its molecules repulsed by,
but drawing closer to, one another; sluggish,
all light cut
from its core. Do fish live,

or weeds, does the snapping turtle sleep
through this? Implacably,
it moves, inch by inch,
hauling another winter in its soul,
hauling grief, the hit-and-run
child's blood, drugged insomnia
of cancer wards, all the small

and bitter dreams of revenge.
All that's crushed,
numb: cruel glacier, ugly
to the silt and sludge. — And which way,
where to, toward which warmer,
wider, bottomless gulf
does it run?

HAITIAN CADAVERS

Harvard, Yale, don't have problems getting bodies,
ditto other prestigious medical colleges,
but lesser schools sometimes need corpses bad

to do their grim and vital work: you can't use one
more than once. And Haitian cadavers
are best for what cadavers do best: lie still

on the anatomical table for the will-be doctors
to dissect. Once the import
problems (practical: fish-chilling chambers

of decommissioned fishing boats; legal: few
precedents) are solved, the deal is good,
the deal is visionary: $50.00 — American — per stiff,

the supply solid, never dwindling, and the topper
that makes it so smooth — a too true
capital dream — is the condition

of the corpses: so thin, all so thin
that the organs just beneath the skin, the organs
yield to the blade with amazing ease.

WALT WHITMAN'S BRAIN DROPPED
ON LABORATORY FLOOR

At his request, after death, his brain was removed
for science, phrenology, to study, and
as the mortuary assistant carried it (I suppose
in a jar but I hope cupped
in his hands) across the lab's stone floor, he dropped it.

You could ask a forensic pathologist
what that might look like. He willed his brain,
as I said, for study — its bumps and grooves,
analyzed, allowing a deeper grasp
of human nature, potential (so phrenology believed),
and this kind of intense look, as opposed to mere fingering

of the skull's outer ridges, valleys, would afford
particular insight. So Walt believed.
He had already scored high (between a 6 and a 7) for Ego.
And as if we couldn't guess from his verses, he scored
high again (a 6 and a 7 — 7 the highest possible!)

in Amativeness (sexual love) and Adhesiveness
(friendship, brotherly love) when before his death
his head was read. He earned only a 5 for Poetic Faculties,
but that 5, pulled and pushed by his other numbers,
allowed our father of poesy to lay down some words
in the proper order on the page. That our nation

does not care does not matter, much.
That his modest federal job was taken from him,
and thus his pension, does not matter at all.
And that his brain was dropped and shattered, a cosmos,
on the floor, matters even less.

UPON SEEING AN ULTRASOUND PHOTO
OF AN UNBORN CHILD

Tadpole, it's not time yet to nag you
about college (though I have some thoughts
on that), baseball (ditto), or abstract
principles. Enjoy your delicious,
soupy womb-warmth, do some rolls and saults
(it'll be too crowded soon), delight in your early
dreams — which no one will attempt to analyze.
For now: may your toes blossom, your fingers
lengthen, your sexual organs grow (too soon
to tell which yet) sensitive, your teeth
form their buds in their forming jawbone, your already
booming heart expand (literally
now, metaphorically later); O your spine,
eyebrows, nape, knees, fibulae,
lungs, lips . . . But your soul,
dear child: I don't see it here, when
does that come in, whence? Perhaps God,
and your mother, and even I — we'll all contribute
and you'll learn yourself to coax it
from wherever: your soul, which holds your bones
together and lets you live
on earth. — Fingerling, sidecar, nubbin,
I'm waiting, it's me, Dad,
I'm out here. You already know
where Mom is. I'll see you more directly
upon arrival. You'll recognize
me — I'll be the tall-seeming, delighted
blond guy, and I'll have
your nose.

BODO

History is largely made of Bodos.
         — Eileen Power, *Medieval People*

We could weep for him
but we won't: the man
who scythed and ground the oats
but ate no bread; who pumped one oar
among thousands at Lepanto, ocean
up to his clavicles and rising; who
in countless numbers served as food
for countless fish. The man,
or sometimes woman, three or four rows back
in the crowd (listless, slack-mouthed),
who lined the street when an army,
depleted or fat with loot, came home;
or the man behind such columns,
who gathered the dung
to sell or to pick for seeds. All the pig farmers,
rat catchers, charcoal burners, tanners
in their stink, root diggers living
in the next village over from the smallest village;
who thickened their soup with sawdust
or meal gathered from dirt
around the grindstone.
Your great-great-etc.-uncle Fedor who never spoke
but in grunts, who beat his spavined horse,
who beat his rented field
for millet, sorghum, who ate a chicken once a year,
who could not read
nor even sign an *X;* the slaves
unnamed who never made it
to the slavers, buzzards' bait,
or did not survive the crossing
if they did. All the Bodos
who stood on docks with breaking backs
and did not wave
and did not know Marco Polo
was setting out again; the zealous priest

eleventh on the list
to seek out Prester John; the convict-colonists
who preferred the gaol at home
but had no choice. The slug-pickers;
the sailors who bailed the bilge water
hanging by their heels; the doughboy
dead of typhus before he wrote a letter home;
the man who thought he pleased a minor Nazi
with an act of small servility
and was proud and told his wife and son;
who lost a leg and half his face for his king,
and then was cheated on his pension
and was not bitter. The man, the woman, who hanged
or burned for nothing
and did not weep, or, tortured, confessed
too fast or less; who praised his slop
in which a fish head floated. . . .

The week waiting for you to be born I read
three books. One, about a dictator so venal as to rip
your soul apart, and his wife, more venal,
who stole and stole and then bought quantities
of what means nothing (jewels, clothes)
in the same way a starving shark
feeds: a frenzy of greed. The second book,
about an African tribe so famished and ill-spirited
they snatched food — literally, gleefully — from the mouths
of their grandparents. And the third book,
on a stern religion
in which a father feels little joy
at a daughter's birth because, ultimately,
she will go to another man, another family,
thereby diminishing his.
It was a normal week of reading: the books I like
are filled with facts.

— Against which there are few options: fragile,
unprofitable love, an insistence,
a fierce, arrogant insistence
toward truth, tolerance, sanity, and a refusal
to self-congratulate for seeking the same.

Earlier, during the day of the night
you were born, I lay down with my face,
my chest, for a while, to the sun, and I slept
and dreamed but not of you. You were nothing
then; you were under water but not drowned,
a contradiction I loved. You were an abstraction.
despite your heartbeat, which I'd heard,
despite the eerie photos — your hazy, huge head,
your tiny pre-body settled
into the curvature of the womb.
I did not dream of you, I dreamed
of what we all always dream of: ourselves,
and in the dream something's just

out of reach, I need it and, frantic, can't
get there. I've had the dream a hundred times: lost
but not lost, calling out but no one hears,
safety, comfort visible across a river,
a river of knives, the bridge made of thread.

— Against which: only anvil-heavy drugs,
which are worse than the dreams,
which crush but don't remove the fear;
only a spirit-thirst — private or public — or knowing,
from within the dream, that you will wake.

In the hours, minutes, before and after
you were born, in the same building
where you and others like you were being born
(I heard their and their mothers' birth-cries,
just as I heard yours and your mother's),
families a few floors down or in the wing opposite
sat weeping around bedsides,
a doctor put her hand gently on a man's shoulder,
a heretofore jumping, jagged line on a screen went flat,
there were gaping chest wounds. . . .
I saw a man in the elevator going home
but knowing it was not for long. I saw tubes of blood
in the technician's rack
on the way to the lab where the malignancy,
the death virus, gets marked on a chart.
So many, like you, go in not existing and leave
otherwise. So many, like all of us, go in existing
and otherwise leave.

— Against which: alas, I'm sorry, that's the way
it . . . the actuaries love to figure
as best they can when; against which: hard cheese,
little ignorant one, big ignorant ones;
against which, my apologies: zero, nada, cipher, nil.

The next day, the day after you were born,
I read a newspaper: someone is riding
a bicycle backward a thousand miles
to promote peace and/or raise money
for a disease; the review of a movie making millions
is headlined "Brainless Exploitation"; religious
leaders, government leaders, commit breathtaking
acts of mendacity, perjury; a vagrant
self-immolates; "Continued Prosperity
Forecast for N.E."; entered into rest
a long alphabetical list (including several
younger than your father!); "China Said
to Caution Japan on Militarism" (again);
a bulldozer, 45k, for sale,
a stonecrusher, hardly used, puppies. . . .
The daily fare, every day ugly in some way,
every day beautiful and gone.

— Against which: no, not always
against or else the bitter grinding, daughter,
the bitter grinding leaves you nothing, nor no will
to go forth, to go forth — in one hand the rage
I hope you have, in the other the rapture.

I like the paintings by the Venetian painters
(Titian, say, or Tintoretto, the Bellinis)
in question: large, dramatic canvases,
figurative (no abstract monkey business here),
relentlessly biblical. The Bible tells
a story, allegory, these guys paint it. Nice. Aside
from beauty, there's a purpose
to this work: people look, they've heard,
or sometimes read, the Bible stories
and they understand them better — the pictorial,
no doubt about it, is powerful. Words

about some gruesome (Christ on the Cross, thorns,
spikes splitting cartilage, spear,
vinegar-sponge in spearhole) or uplifting
(Resurrection) scene
are all right, but an image — there it is,
friend, that's what it looked like — better still.
The less than literal touches I like best,
however, in so many of these: the chubby,
ubiquitous, usually just hovering
above and/or back a bit
from the central tableau (we can see them,

but can the characters in the picture?) rosy fellows
with wings; joyous, busy,
observational little blimps, their delicate wings
not flapping (never painted as a blur
despite their weight), but there they fly, floating

babies! For centuries
they show up — sometimes carrying a lyre,
a dove or two, of course a bow,
but mostly just ecstatic, naked, fat.
Bless them, their cargo,
their unexampled flight patterns.

The basic metaphor is good: blend dead,
redolent things — dried blood,
steamed bone meal, dried hoof and horn
meal, slag, dolomite,
bat guano — into the dirt,
wait; live things will emerge.
In between, of course, you insert a seed.
So fragile, at first — I examine rows
of lettuce seedlings with a reading glass,
their green so barely green
they break your heart. The only
tools you need are Stone Age
but made of metal: I love
the shovel's cut when you plunge
it in: the shiny, smooth cliff-face
and some worms (your garden's pals!)
in the middle of their bodies,
their lives, divided. . . . A rake,
a hoe, peasant tools,
but mostly you pick, pull, pinch by hand,
the green stains and stinks clinging
to your fingertips.
Don't read books about it,
or not many. Turn the dirt
and comb it smooth.
Plant what you like to eat.
Feed the birds — but not so much
that they get lazy —
and they will eat the bugs,
who should get their share,
but not one leaf of basil more.
It's all a matter of spirit, balance,
common cruel sense: something dies,
something's born, and, in the meantime,
you eat some salad.

All whom I love, all neighbors
and relations awry and pure, all intimates
of the same heart-paths, all strangers I would know
would want to go there,
would be compelled
thusward: the most northern,
unknown, uninvented, patchy, unvisited spot
on the maps. And I
would go with them. In shivering boats,
leaky carracks, floats
of reed and gum, or llama train
overland. . . . No charts
or longitude (dead
reckoning our trust in thee) — just impudent
and greedy to leave the greedy,
fleeing the murder figurative,
literal. It's no longer listed,
Ultima Thule, on the maps or indexes: too many
set out to fill it in — Ellesmere
Island, Baffin, Meta
Incognita Peninsula, Boothia Felix. . . .
They went for fur and gold,
or to find the westward road
to East: for fur and gold. — Still, we would go there,
around the globe, until it opens
to another sphere,
a land unplumbed, a queer place
where we, the new skraelings,
the happy natives, where we
could welcome our winter wheat
and haul the summer fishes
from the cold salt sea.

I have a friend whose hair is like time: dark
deranged coils lit by a lamp
when she bends back her head to laugh. A unique event,
such as the crucifixion of Christ, was not
subject to repetition, thought St. Augustine, and therefore
time is linear. Does the universe
have an end, a beginning? Yes, the former the door
through which she departs, the latter
the door by which she returns,
and in between there is no rest from wanting her.

Time — each moment of which a hair on a child's nape.
Time — the chain between the churning tractor and the stump.
Time — her gown tossed like a continent at the Creation.
Newton, an absolutist, thought time a container
in which the universe exists — nonending, nonbeginning.
Time — enamored, forgiven by dust,
and capable of calling a single blade of grass an oasis.
Time — of swivel, small streams, plinth, stanchions.
And then Kant says no, time does not apply
to the universe, only to the way we think about time.

Time — the spot where the violin touches the maestro's cheek.
Time — an endless range of cumulonimbus.
Time — Good Monarch of the deepest blue inevitable.
The relativists (with whom the absolutists,
as usual, disagree) argue that concepts of past,
present, and future are mind-dependent, i.e.,
would time exist without conscious beings?
O Ultimate Abstract, is there time
in time, is there rest, in time,
from wanting her?

THE SUDD AS METAPHOR

Malarial, malodorous, papyrus-choked
sump (250 mi. x 50 mi.!) impeding those who sought
the Source, the Nile's, for decades. An inland Sargasso
neither land nor water, with no past and no present,
the few channels through (Lake No,
River of Giraffes) often closed, or they'd, worse,
lead you in, then close. A million
browns, greens — mosses, water lettuce,
coarse grasses decayed, compressed by currents

into peat-like blocks, strong enough to walk on,
hop across (to lead you in), strong
enough at times to hold an elephant
but not too long before it takes him under,
his trunk like a two-eyed periscope the last to slip
beneath the tepid ooze.
The Source impeded, no further advancement
toward the Source! Boats under
sail, oar, steam — blocked

for weeks, months, hacking
with billhooks forward, the foetid air
hanging sodden in sheets: dysentery, mosquitoes,
starvation, madness. The Source denied,
not given over, for decades,
until inch by inch a channel carved,
bitten, sawed — hundreds die in so doing — through,
and it is open, a thin passage,
it is open, agape.

WHAT I SEE WHEN I DRIVE TO WORK

(Boston to New York)

On clear days it's fast black dead west sixty miles
New England blazing or granite-brown
on both sides of the slide. Then a dip south-
west — the sun on my left cheek now flat
on my chest, and I'm warm,
with the other citizens, driving
to work. About lunchtime

I hit Hartford (each week a honk
for Wallace Stevens) — half a day done
for the insurance clerks and I'm halfway
to work. Twenty or so miles later,
on the arc of a long dropping curve, the sun
takes a quarry's gouged-out bowl.
I like the big machines, drills

and dozers, that eat
the rock and break it down to sand — at least
more than I like the insurance industry;
and then a town's announced
by a giant Jesus' coat rack
on a rubbled hill. It overlooks
a happy, placid burg known for brass

where I never stop
for gas or sandwich. I'm driving
to work — talk radio/gun control, Squantz
Pond, lunch pail, Ruby Road, never-cross-
a-picket-line, on my way
to earn a wage: Massachusetts, Connecticut,
and now nudging into New York,

just over which border
I follow for a few miles a river
that opens to a lake
that each day this fall
is open to more and more ducks,
which makes me happy, at this point,
driving to work with the rest of America,

who mostly get there before I do.
The last leg's most scenic, woodsy,
and takes me past a publishing complex,
Reader's Digest, Inc., massive buildings
on a hill, where a man someday
might reduce this poem to haiku.
I'm nearing now and exit by the exit

by the blind school — two more miles,
if I take the shortcut past some mansions,
to my office, which is
199.4 mi.
from my home. It's a lengthy motoring,
but the work is honest
and the customers human.

says Audrey to herself in the mirror, adjusting
her lemon-colored scarf,
dabbing a little scent behind her ears,
opening her robe to pat a drop or two
between her breasts (where else might there be
a pulse? she wonders). Painfully banal,
she says again, this time out loud and making sure

not to offend her image, adding, Not you, darling,
not you, I'm referring to Bernard. Bernard,
meanwhile, is on the balcony, framed
by the French doors, thinking, as authors do,
about his novel. *There is a sousaphone
on the glass coffee table.* He mouths
this opening, and thus far only, sentence, delighting

in the $\overline{oo}$ sound, how it contrasts nicely
with the later harsher adenoidal (*glăs, kôfē*)
sounds: The range of a novelist,
he thinks, the ear of a poet! P.B.B. — Painfully
Banal Bernard, Audrey
says out loud, snapping her fists apart,
drawing her dressing gown tighter around her waist.

A LITTLE TOOTH

Your baby grows a tooth, then two,
and four, and five, then she wants some meat
directly from the bone. It's all

over: she'll learn some words, she'll fall
in love with cretins, dolts, a sweet
talker on his way to jail. And you,

your wife, get old, flyblown, and rue
nothing. You did, you loved, your feet
are sore. It's dusk. Your daughter's tall.

BLACK ROAD OVER WHICH
GREEN TREES GROW

A tunnel, but the roof is green and some light
breaks through. There's lots
of oxygen; no worms eat
the leaves or your lungs.
On this road coffins in hearses have been
passing through, not parked or stalled.
On this road: wedding party, friendships, family
visits, a childhood summer sunk
in hot asphalt; dead pets, the broken
white line a monotonous Morse code: help,

help, help. How long this road,
which side streets glimpsed, which streetlamps
shattered, mailbox tilted?
On this road: forever-for-sale house, a vacant
lot's weeds rasping (were they ever
alive?), half-masted
by wind. No other car, never,
neither ahead nor behind, no
human — mailman, milkman, child
behind a lemonade stand. No road

signs: Rte. Such and Such, So and So-ville 4 mi.,
X-ton Lions Club Welcomes You. . . . Just
this tunnel road, this chute,
this track driven down in silence
(no radio reception), alone, so many thousand
times and you do
not stop, you do
not die, you just drive out
the other side,
you just drive on out the other side.

MR. POPE

Do you think I would not wish to have been
friends with such a man as this?
— Charles Lamb

Life on earth,
for Mr. Pope, was not lenient: four foot six, hunch-
backed, grinding migraines,
hard-to-breathe, deep bone aches,
and, most likely, never, *never*
any sex. That he did not
tolerate nincompoops,
poetasters, or pompous fops
one can understand.
It was not meanness or misanthropy
that drove him to ravage dunces
but more so sorrow
and some rage. Attacks on his work part of the deal
(*a very pretty poem,*
Mr. Pope, but you must not call it Homer),
he could take, but attacks upon his body (*a lump,*
a toad, a venomous spider,
a monkey dropping filth) compounded the pain.
The censure he dealt almost always
earned, rarely the spirit mean,
or mere spleen. And toward those
he loved: tremendous affection, generous.
Mr. Pope, thou giant,
your tubercular bacillus-wracked body, now,
a quarter millennium later, powder,
and I report your verses,
their raging sense
and tenderness, I report
them breathing, shining black
ink on white paper, intact!
I close the heavy, huge book of your life.
You live outside, above, its pages,
within the human therein created.

The hard hook-finger clutching down to the bottom
of the belly, all
nerve-roots awash, aswirl
with want this, want this, and this
over and over against the wharf's eaten pillars.
Tides of this . . . this fearful need, avalanches

of it, typhoons, tsunami followed by tsunami,
dogged. What is it beats the engine,
rips with a thong the donkey's flank raw,
what lament-drenched trek
so hard in comparison diamond is cream?
To what end, purpose, to serve

what obsession the kindergarten
teacher moonlighting as gravedigger, the heiress
taking in laundry, the priest
wearing beneath his vestments satanic tattoos?
What is it drives it? Sex? *Love me, love me*
over and over, that? Or money,

just money — *give me that, if I have
this I* . . . Is it money,
is that why the soul reaches out with pincers
after what is outside the soul?
What is it, how to make it palpable?

Is it the old thing, the cave-man thing,
maybe even the monkey thing: fear
of nothingness which even the philosophers
cannot make go away: *don't die, don't
die?* What creates the purpose,
what fuel, what feeds the fire
in the skull?

THE PERFECT GOD

The perfect god puts forth no dogma, cant,
or laws that dim the soul. He lets you sleep
and eat and work and love and treats you like
a man, woman. He needs no slaves; the self-
appointed, meek but cruel — they annoy him.
There are old books he didn't write but likes

for their rhythms and truths some of the stories tell.
He likes, loves these books, I said, but is bored
by exegesis too literal, wild.
Prose, poems, sometimes suffer the same fate,
but this also bores him and he won't, can't,
or does not care, or dare, to interfere

with either. The perfect god is sad, hurt,
when humans fear their lives — those solitudes
so small beside the tundra, polar caps,
Congo River (whose every curve he loves),
the empty, equatorial bliss. He likes,
loves what's vast, which seems to us so blank.

He loves what's sane, serene, and fiercely calm,
which he didn't invent but understands.
The perfect god — and god, yes, is perfect —
is impassive, patient, aloof, alert,
and needs not our praise nor our blame.
And needs not our praise nor our blame.

why there are black half-donuts beneath each eye
in the mirror: bad sleep, drug
sleep; why the president's shrug
maims 1,004 children each hour: he has taken from them
childhood and lunch; why fashion,
as in clothes (the sullen, bored models
believe themselves perceptibly aging
between clicks of the camera), matters, I can
explain: *In democratic societies*
each citizen is habitually busy with the contemplation

of a very petty object, which is himself.
I can explain cruelty: fear.
I can explain greed: fear of death.
I can explain love: fear of death and fear.
I can explain a tunnel
at the bottom of a pit
in the corner of a cave
in the plumbless depths of a heart: nobody home,
no human ever lived there.
I can explain where I was when I was supposed

to be with someone good doing something
decent: I was somewhere else
with someone bad
doing something not decent.
I can explain the need to turn
and turn pages filled with marks
made by the dead . . . no I can't, yes
I can, no I can't. And finally, I can explain
the meaning, the desideratum
of it all, the quota of gasps

tossed daily into graves, the longing
toward the rare underbelly of mink,
the guilt and the peace
calm as milk or chalk, I can explain it all
by tilting back my head
and opening my mouth to the rain,
the starlight, tomorrow's brilliant snow,
each brave flake
not cold
but alone.

Major progress is: in the act of embracing ourselves
we do not do so because of cold, fear,
but out of absolute — which is healthy,
the magazines say — self-love, which is healthy,
a positive self-image is *healthy,*

all the experts say,
and less effort
than loving an other. I am I, therefore
I am good: love thyself
selflessly, that's OK. And if

you want me, or want me
to want you, or want to
sell me something, then tell me
I'm beautiful. If there is a blank anywhere
in your life, an abyss tucked high up behind your breast bone,

or a black molecule of doubt
in your soul, well then,
fill in that blank,
palimpsest that abyss, that doubt with optimism: you can!
In the mirror in the morning say

this: *I like* my*self.* This
is your iambic dimeter mantra, say it,
and all the rest that diminishes you
will disappear down the bones of your face,
will die all night outside your door,

will file away like a line of ants.
Say it, say it: I'm beautiful,
I'm loved — and then wager it all,
all of the ice, all of it,
on the ice to win.

Blind wind beats the bushes down and wild,
like the hair of the mad: it's a day, a page
ripped from a book of childhood — yours, any child's,
it's a moment when all is clear, changed.

And it is always on a day of chill and rain, a fierce
gray frame to everything. A stained huddle of cows
bellows in the barnyard: *Let us in,* their eyes pierced
by pain, dumbness. And the child watches. How

do these moments, these fractures in time
happen, how is a child taken, struck
by something . . . something, taken low or high,
filled with world or forever with self? Is it luck,

good or bad? One child hears a falling through the leaves,
branches, and does not care what it is,
another hears and *knows* a bird falls, and grieves
without knowing why or at what cost. This

one is the winter child, the one so filled with world.
The other, no better, no less (neither has a choice),
through his life is obliviously hurled.
You hear him talking but it doesn't seem like a voice.

The wind rips across the damp and freezing pastures,
children fill the schoolyards, the shattered towns,
and the stars expel their light — last year's,
last millennium's, their gelid light drilling down.

from

SPLIT
HORIZON

1994

hate the people of this village
and would nail our hats
to our heads for refusing in their presence to remove them
or staple our hands to our foreheads
for refusing to salute them
if we did not hurt them first: mail them packages of rats,
mix their flour at night with broken glass.
We do this, they do that.
They peel the larynx from one of our brothers' throats.
We devein one of their sisters.
The quicksand pits they built were good.
Our amputation teams were better.
We trained some birds to steal their wheat.
They sent to us exploding ambassadors of peace.
They do this, we do that.
We canceled our sheep imports.
They no longer bought our blankets.
We mocked their greatest poet
and when that had no effect
we parodied the way they dance
which did cause pain, so they, in turn, said our God
was leprous, hairless.
We do this, they do that.
Ten thousand (10,000) years, ten thousand
(10,000) brutal, beautiful years.

The thing gets made, gets built, and you're the slave
who rolls the log beneath the block, then another,
then pushes the block, then pulls a log
from the rear back to the front
again and then again it goes beneath the block,
and so on. It's how a thing gets made — not
because you're sensitive, or you get genetic-lucky,
or God says: Here's a nice family,
seven children, let's see: this one in charge
of the village dunghill, these two die of buboes, this one
Kierkegaard, this one a drooling

nincompoop, this one clerk, this one cooper.
You need to love the thing you do — birdhouse building,
painting tulips exclusively, whatever — and then
you do it
so consciously driven
by your unconscious
that the thing becomes a wedge
that splits a stone and between the halves
the wedge then grows, i.e., the thing
is solid but with a soul,
a life of its own. Inspiration, the donnée,

the gift, the bolt of fire
down the arm that makes the art?
Grow up! Give me, please, a break!
You make the thing because you love the thing
and you love the thing because someone else loved it
enough to make you love it.
And with that your heart like a tent peg pounded
toward the earth's core.
And with that your heart on a beam burns
through the ionosphere.
And with that you go to work.

GORGEOUS SURFACES

They are, the surfaces, gorgeous: a master
pastry chef at work here, the dips and whorls,
the wrist-twist
squeezes of cream from the tube
to the tart, sweet bleak sugarwork, needlework
towards the perfect lace doily
where sit the bone china teacups, a little maze
of meaning maybe in their arrangement,
sneaky obliques, shadow
allusives all piling
atop one another. Textures succulent but famished,
banal, bereft. These surfaces,
these flickering patinas,
these gorgeous surfaces
through which,
if you could drill, or hack,
or break a trapdoor latch, if you could penetrate
these surfaces' milky cataracts, you
would drop,
free fall
like a hope chest full of lead,
to nowhere, no place, a dry-wind, sour,
nada place,
and you would keep dropping,
tumbling, slow
motion, over and over for one day, six days, fourteen
decades, eleven centuries (a long time
falling to fill a zero), and in that time
not a leaf, no rain,
not a single duck, nor hearts, not one human, nor sleep,
nor grace, nor graves — falling
to where the bottom, finally, is again the surface,
which is gorgeous,
which is glue, saw- and stone-dust, which is blue-gray
ice, which is
the barely glinting grit of abyss.

Rabbit tracks in an inch or so of new snow
have no origin (for who
follows tracks backwards?)
and have no end (the rabbit forever
moving ahead or disappears
into a swamp). You pick
them up behind the corncrib, follow north
along the fenceline where he stopped, shook
a few seed pods off some dry weeds,
left some droppings (either because he had to

or to mark a territory: these are *my*
seeds, grim as they are, these are *mine*)
and then he cut due west, his straightest line yet,
across a pasture, exposed, his tracks wider,
running. A lean time, February,
for rabbits. He half-slid down a slit ravine,
his rump making a trough
through his tracks. Over
the small brook's center not frozen over
he must have leapt: deft

rabbit, hungry rabbit.
Then under the fallen bottom strand of barbwire
(a small tuft of gray-brown fur
points south on a north wind)
and into brush so thick
you cannot enter, though you try, a few yards.
You never saw him: ditto.
He never saw you: ditto.
And all the tracks behind ahead overblown by a new inch
of snow: dot, dot, ditto.

VIRGULE

What I love about this little leaning mark
is how it divides
without divisiveness. The left
or bottom side prying that choice up or out,
the right or top side pressing down upon
its choice: either/or,
his/her. Sometimes called a slash (too harsh), a slant
(a little dizzy but the Dickinson association
nice: "Tell the truth but tell it slant"), a solidus (sounding
too much like a Roman legionnaire
of many campaigns),
or a separatrix (reminding one of a sexual
variation). No, I like virgule. I like the word
and I like the function: "Whichever is appropriate
may be chosen to complete the sense."
There is something democratic
about that, grown-up; a long
and slender walking stick set against the house.
Virgule: it feels good in your mouth.
Virgule: its foot on backwards, trochaic, that's OK, American.
Virgule: you could name your son that,
or your daughter, Virgula. I'm sorry now
I didn't think to give my daughter such a name
though I doubt that she and/or
her mother would share that thought.

To go there: do not fall asleep, your forehead
on the footstool; do not have
your lunchpail dreams
or dreams so peaceful you hear leaves thud
into the fine silt at a river's edge;
do not hope you'll find it on this updraft
or that downdraft
in the airy airlessness.
It is elsewhere, elsewhere, the neighborhood you seek.
The neighborhood you long for,
where the gentle trolley — *ding, ding* — passes
through, where the adults are kind
and, better, sane,
that neighborhood is gone, no, never
existed, though it should have
and had a chance once
in the hearts of women, men (farmers dreamed
this place, and teachers, book writers, oh thousands
of workers, mothers prayed for it, hunchbacks,
nurses, blind men, maybe most of all soldiers,
even a few generals, millions
through the millennia . . .), some of whom,
despite anvils on their chests,
despite taking blow after blow across shoulders and necks,
despite derision and scorn,
some of whom still, *still*
stand up every day against ditches swollen with blood,
against ignorance, still dreaming,
full-fledged adults, still fighting,
trying to build a door to that place,
trying to pry open the ugly,
bullet-pocked, and swollen gate
to the other side,
the neighborhood of make-believe.

EDGAR ALLAN POE MEETS SARAH HALE
(AUTHOR OF "MARY HAD A LITTLE LAMB")

One would assume a difference in temperaments.
Their introduction likely took place at a lit'ry salon,
common in their day — Poe looking past her
at the punch bowl — or possibly they met
at the offices of *Godey's Lady's Book,* of which Sarah Hale
was an editor and for which
she purchased several stories (including
"The Purloined Letter") and sketches.
Because she knew — everybody knew — he needed cash
she paid him less than other authors,
knowing he'd take it. Business.
Nevertheless, Poe thought highly
enough of Hale to write: . . . *a lady of fine genius*
and masculine energy and ability.
Was he aware of his patronizing? Unlikely.
Was he being obsequious? More likely.
He needed the money, being a drunk
and with a large laudanum habit.
Sarah Hale wrote a poem we all know.
The same is true for Mr. Edgar Allan Poe.

We were in a room that was once an attic,
tops of trees filled the windows, a breeze
crossed the table where we sat
and Amiel, about age four, came to visit
with her father, my friend,
and it was spring I think, and I remember
being happy — her mother was there too,
and my wife, and a few other friends.
It was spring, late spring, because the trees
were full but still that slightly lighter
green; the windows were open,
some of them, and I'll say it
out loud: I was happy, sober, at the time childless
myself, and it was one
of those moments: just like that, Amiel
climbed on my lap and put her head back against my chest.
I put one hand on her knees
and my other hand on top of that hand.
That was all, that was it.
Amiel's leg was cool, faintly rubbery.
We were there — I wish I knew the exact
date, time — and that
was all, that was it.

If I mix a vegetable and moral metaphor
then this pale,
arrogant little leaf— its juices spare,
its taste pinched
and numbing — is equivalent
to a rich child pulling legs
off a bug, to a swaggering walk through a TB ward
by a pulmonary giant. Not to mention
a pathetic excuse for salad: four, five spiked shards
arranged like spokes
around its hub: a radish delicately carved.
The white plate upon which it sits so bare it blinds me.
Who, forced to wear white butler's gloves,
bends over a row all day
to pick this for a lousy wage
and can't afford or, I'd prefer, refuses
to eat it? It's so pallid
turning to yellow, I feel stabbing it
with my fork
would hurt it
or at least be impolite
so I slide the shiny tines beneath a piece
and lift it to my lips
and it's as if I'm eating air
but with a slight afterburn: dust and bone,
privilege and toe dancing.
So delicate, curling in on itself
in an ultimate self-embrace: fussy, bitter, chaste, clerical
little leaf.

FRANKLY, I DON'T CARE

This miserable scene demands a groan.
— John Gay

Frankly, I don't care if the billionaire is getting divorced
and thus boosting the career
of his girlfriend, a "model/spokesperson" with no job
and nothing to promote; nor does my concern
over celebrity X undergoing surgical procedures,
leaked as "primarily cosmetic" if it can be measured
quantitatively, reach the size of the space
inside a hollow needle. Regardless,
prayer vigils are being held
around the clock in the hospital lobby.
It's not that I wish
for a slip of the surgeon's wrist
but I just flat-simple don't care
although I understand and try
to empathize: as beauty diminishes
so does the bankroll. I am also indifferent
to — to the point of yawns large enough
to swallow the world — a senator's or, say, singer's
girlfriend's or boyfriend's disclosures
re the singer's or senator's sexual behavior — well, unless
the disclosure is *explicitly* detailed
and for christsake *interesting!*
— But does this protest too much?
We the people, day-laboring citizens, need to love
those of you larger than us, those whose teeth
are like floodlights against loneliness,
whose great gifts of song, or for joke telling,
or thespianly sublime transformations
take us, for whole moments at a time, away
from ourselves. We need
you and from this point on we promise
to respect your privacy,
diminish our demands on you,
never to take pleasure
in your troubles or pain.

And on those cruel days when death has its way
and takes two or even three of you
at once, three of more or less equal fame, we will,
in the obituaries, the newscasts, the front pages,
we will list your departures alphabetically;
your popularity will not, on this day, be tallied
or polled. Because in death, although still not anonymous,
you will be like us: small,
equal, voiceless, and gone.

THE DRIVER ANT

Eats meat exclusively. Can't bear
direct sunlight, marches at night,
in tall grass, or in covered causeways
it builds, by day. Relentless,
nervous, short, conservative,
twenty million or more,
like a thick black living rope
they exit, often, the colony
to eat: lizards, guanas, monkeys,
rats, mice, the tasty
largest python, *Python natelensis,*
who just devoured a small antelope
and can't move: double dinner,
in a few hours a pile of bones
inside a pile of bones.
This army's slow
(one meter per three min.) so
they can't catch you
unless you're lame,
or dumb, or staked
to the ground — a hard way to die,
eating first your eyes,
and then too many mandibles
clean you to your spine.
The Driver Ant, penniless,
goes out to eat
in hordes, in rivers, in armies of need,
good citizens
serving a famished state.

The patient children stand in line
to be counted, to be assigned
their seats by height: the short up front,
taller to the rear. November, frozen puddles
shine like the eyes of a somnambulist
if you lift his lids. Needle wind.
The Nazi, a dead-serious
doorkeeper, a functionary

at the puppet show,
takes the tickets, slow,
up and down the line
and tears each one
at the angle of a guillotine
but will not let the children in.
They do not wail or whine.
They're here to see the show in which the rabbit

outwits the crocodile and is not
eaten. To see that, they will bear a lot.
The Nazi blocks the door, checks her watch.
Inside, over a candle,
the puppeteer warms his hands.
And the puppets lie as still and blind
as wood, as buttons, as cloth
in their blue-black box.

were really one problem: the God he chose
was capricious, cruel, cold,
and a windbag, yammer, yammer,
a fine poet (or his ghostwriter) but a windbag,
braggart. Hurt, He said,
hurt Job terribly,
kill (and they need not
be mentioned again) his ten children,
pile boil upon boil upon his back,
program the locust to gnaw away his nose,
but don't
let him die, I'll want to rub some salt in
later. . . . Not death,
just torture: now there's a God
to whom you want to give your heart.
As Maimonides said: Job was a good man,
but stupid. As were his friends Bildad,
Eliphaz, and Zophar: boneheads,
mewly aphorists, boot lickers, greeting card
optimists, and them too — yammer, yammer.
And Job had some breath to expend himself,
a gift for metaphor,
simile. Also ego
and self-effacement (where is the latter
really the former?), and then God,
insecure, piqued,
deigns to speak
from within a whirlwind
and is, of course, the better poet
though his work flawed by arrogance
and also too oblique.
Maybe he's more afraid of being understood,
as Nietzsche said
of certain philosophers,
than he is of being *mis*understood.
Job, nevertheless, is impressed, submits.

God, his ego salved,
first rebukes Bildad, Eliphaz, and Zophar
(no protest from them), then
gives back, twofold, Job's sheep, camels, cows,
provides seven new sons and three new daughters,
daughters very beautiful
and with very exotic names,
not Joan, or Betty, or Jane.
And, God gave Job
the famous 140 more years
(on top of how many already?), which means
he outlived his wife
and second family
and died rich, and happy, and alone.

KALASHNIKOV

*(an AK-47 assault rifle, probably the most
numerous small-arms weapon in history)*

Designed by Mikhail Kalashnikov who, if alive
today, is seventy-three years old,
but is he
as well known in his native Russia
as Marina Tsvetayeva, Anna Akhmatova,
or Osip Mandelstam? Russians love
their poets. I don't know

how they feel about Kalashnikov
but he is or was wealthier
than the poets above ever were
and has out there several million
of his namesakes: read a book
in which people shoot people — revolutionaries,
whether earnest, sincere,

or just thugs: Kalashnikovs, everybody's got one.
There's a guerrilla
somewhere: a Kalashnikov. Assassins,
warlords' soldiers, smugglers, pirates,
poachers: Kalashnikovs, caliber
7.62 x 39, 600 rounds
per minute, a potential 10 corpses

per second.
Kalashnikov — it's not a dance,
nor a troupe of funny jugglers,
nor is it a vodka,
and if you said a small city (pop. 49,000)
in the southern Crimea,
you'd be stone-dead wrong.

MONEY

A paper product. We say it's green
but it's not, it's slate green, drained green.
New, it smells bad
but we like to sniff it
and when we have a relative pile
we not only want to inhale it but also look at it,
hear it buzz
as we work with our thumbs
its corners like a deck of cards.
A wall of it would be nice, in bricks
like you see in the movies
when vaults get robbed.
And those beautiful — so tiny — red, blue threads,
capillaries, cilia, embedded
in the texture of the paper (that secret
which most thwarts the phony money men),
those threads
like river valleys on a distant planet,
rivers with no end, no source,
like steep ravines in an otherwise flat pan
of a landscape. Look long
and deep enough
at a piece of paper money
and you will see the heaven you were promised,
there, which we look so hard into,
to the very bottom, depths of which
we are called
by the riverbed, the ravine's bleached stones
calling us down: money, money,
paper money.

gets made up of 5.3 billion little pictures (sacks, thousands,
of rice rotting, rat-gnawed, in warehouses, jail cell
graffiti, a tiny crimson powder-burned disc
on a man's forehead, a torturer's migraine, immense
abstract delusions — *no problem here* — a filthy

fingernail sunk in a chunk of gray bread . . .), eleven pictures
of medium size (the Marxist discussion group
breaks down into smaller groups
to study punctuational/syntactical nuances, why nobody
minds lies if they are colossal enough, etc.), a few blank

frames (example: Jesus walking on water and rising
from the dead?, the Mormon guy, Joe Smith — sounds like
an alias — digging up some gold plates
in his backyard?: this enumeration, this list
of mysteries could go on and on

without *ever any* verification . . .), a few ruined
snapshots (a chicken in every BBQ, social justice), one
shattered vision, a few mild
auditory hallucinations, faint harp
music, celestial crowing

or choiring, or the low love cooing
of an amorous duo,
Ignorance and Certainty, that each lost one of us,
I pray, would agree, should agree, should be
sterilized!

This valley: as if a huge, dull, primordial ax
once slammed into the earth
and then withdrew, innumerable millennia ago.
A few flat acres
ribbon either side of the river sliding sluggishly
past the clock tower, the convenience store.
If a river could look over its shoulder,
glad to be going, this one would.
In town center: a factory of clangor and stink,
of grinding and oil,
hard howls from drill bits
biting sheets of steel. All my brothers
live here, every cousin, many dozens
of sisters, my worn aunts
and numb uncles, the many many of me,
a hundred sad wives,
all of us countrymen and -women
born next to each other behind the plow
in this valley, each of us
pressing to our chests a loaf of bread
and a jug of milk. . . . The river is low
this time of year and the bedstones' blackness
marks its lack
of depth. A shopping cart
lies on its side in center stream
gathering branches, detritus, silt,
forcing the already weak current to part for it,
dividing it, but even so diminished
it's glad to be going,
glad to be gone.

First, a female buffalo gnat of the genus *Simulium* bites you
and in the process
deposits her infective larvae.
In ten to twenty months (no big hurry) they grow
to threadlike adult worms
which live up to fifteen years under the skin,
intermuscularly, in fascial planes, against the capsules
of joints or the shafts of long bones — the neighborhoods
they love inside you. The adult females,
now residing in your body, produce live embryos
which live a year or two,
migrating, restless,
during which time they will likely invade your eyes,
lymph glands, or other (you don't want to know
which) organs. Results
are unpleasant: blindness, which might be merciful,
for then you don't see: rash, wheals, gross
lichenification, atrophy (known as "lizard skin"),
enlarged lymph glands
leading to pockets of loose flesh,
"hanging groins," which predispose
to hernia, and so on.
Treatment: Serious drugs, some so toxic the treatment worse
than the illness.
Prognosis: If you are not reinfected, the parasites die out
within fifteen years. Symptoms of disease, however, may
get worse during this time.
Prevention: Avoid Third World communities,
particularly those located within twenty kilometers
of fast-flowing rivers
in which *Simulium* prefers to breed.
Some twenty to forty million (hard to be exact!) people
infected,
baby flies dying, dying
in their eyes,
blinding them.

That is, their authors, leave out
one thing: the smell. How sour, no, rancid — bad cheese
and sweat — the narrow corridors of Hitler's bunker
during the last days powdered
by plaster shaken down
under bomb after bomb. Or (forward or backward
through time, history books take you) downstream
a mile or two from a river-crossing ambush
a corpse washes ashore
or catches in branches
and bloats in the sun. The carrion eaters
who do not fly
come by their noses: the thick,
ubiquitous, sick, sweet smell.
Most of history, however,
is banal, not bloody: the graphite and wood smell
of a pencil factory, the glue- fertilizer- paper-
(oh redolent!) shoe- hat- (ditto malodor
and poisonous) chemical- salt cod–
munitions- canning- shirtwaist- plastics- box-
tractor- etc. factories — and each one
peopled by people: groins, armpits, feet.
A bakery, during famine; guards, smoking, by the door.
Belowdecks, two years out, dead calm, tropics.
And wind a thousand miles all night combing
the tundra: chilled grasses, polar bear droppings,
glacial exhalations. . . . Open
the huge book of the past: *whoosh!*: a staggering cloud
of stinks, musks
and perfumes, swollen pheromones, almond
and anise, offal dumps, mass graves exhumed, flower
heaps, sandalwood bonfires, milk vapors
from a baby's mouth, all of us
wading hip-deep through the endless
waftings, one bottomless soup
of smells: primal, atavistic — sniff, sniff, sniff.

The graveyard being what he called his face;
even as a young man
he called his face the graveyard — he talked
like that, funny, odd
things that scared me sometimes

in our early years. I thought maybe he was a little touched
(his Uncle Bob was certifiable)
but it was just his way of talking. *U-feeisms,*
he told me once, he liked to use *u-feeisms,*
which was no language

I ever heard of. He never touched a drop, though,
nor ever lifted a hand against me
or the kids, and when it came to loving,
well, he was sweet, but talking strange then
too: Bug Sauce, he'd call me, or Lavender Limbs,

or sometimes Birdbath — never Honey
or Sugar like other husbands when they talked, talked.
He was funny like that. Anyway,
after breakfast (he always shaved *after* breakfast,
said his face was "looser" then)

he'd stroke his chin and say:
Time to shave the graveyard,
and he would and then he'd go to work,
the handle of his lunchpail hooked through
with a belt and slung

over his shoulder. Some days I'd watch him
until he reached the corner
of Maple and Cottage
where he turned and walked the two blocks
to the mill.

PECKED TO DEATH BY SWANS

— for Stephen Dobyns

Your tear-wracked family bedside: elderly grandchildren,
great-grandchildren arriving
straight from med school; not a peep of pain, calm,
lucid, last words impeccably drafted?

No. Pecked to death by swans.

Having saved the lives of twelve crippled children
(pulled from a burning circus tent), the president
calling your hospital room, and you say: *Tell him
to call back;* all the opiate drugs you want?

No. Pecked to death by swans.

Great honors accrued, *Don't go* telegram from the pope
on the side table, serious lobby
already in place re a commemorative stamp; a long
long life capped by falling, peacefully, asleep?

No. I said: Pecked to death by swans.

By a bullet meant for a lover or a best friend,
by a car set to kill someone else whom you pushed,
because you could, out of the way; the ululations
of a million mourners rising to your window?

No. Pecked to death by swans.

The minute my brother gets out of jail I want
some answers: when our mother
murdered our father
did she find out first, did he tell her — the pistol's tip
parting his temple's fine hairs — did he
tell her where our sister (the youngest, Alice)
hid the money Grandma (mother's side)
stole from her Golden Age Group?
It was a lot of money but *enough to die for?*
was what Mom said she asked him,
giving him a choice. *I'll see you in hell,*
she said Dad said
and then she said (this is in the trial transcript): *Not
any time soon, needle dick!*
We know Alice hid the money — she was arrested

a week later in Tacoma for armed robbery,
which she would not have done
if she had it. Alice was (she died
of a heroin overdose six hours after making bail)
syphilitic, stupid, and rude
but not greedy. So she hid the money,
or Grandma did,
but since her stroke can't say a word,
doesn't seem to know anybody.
Doing a dime at Dannemora
for an unrelated sex crime, my brother
might know something but won't answer
my letters, refuses to see me,
though he was the one who called me
at divinity school

after Mom was arrested. He could hardly
get the story out from laughing
so much: Dad had missed
his third in a row the day before with his parole officer,
the cops were sent
to pick him up (*Bad timing,* said Mom) and found him
before he was cold.
He was going back to jail anyway, Mom said,
said the cops,
which they could and did use against her
to the tune of double digits, which means,
what with the lupus, she's guaranteed
to die inside. Ask her?
She won't talk to me.
She won't give me the time of day.

THE RIVER THAT SCOLDS
AT ALL THE OTHER RIVERS

This bossy river, its rate of descent a degree or two greater
than its neighbors, its bed
of bigger stones — *Oh rounder, more smooth, it seems*
to say, my alluvium
so much richer — this river is angry now, in spring,
bragging, after a winter of heavy snow
in the mountains. *On I go with more urgency*
than you, it says to the little river that runs parallel
for so many miles, *you will be part of me,*
I will eat you soon. And the smaller river
does, is, that is, becomes a part of it, and the larger
larger, bossier still. *My path*
the best path, my notch, my groove
the most true, says the river, I will
eat my banks, bow my own bends;
the shortest distance between two points,
that's how I go and haul
with me whatever is in my way,
taking it all: the trees, and men
in tissuey canoes, the ice, the rain,
the moon on my back, everything,
louder and louder as I go, the dwellings
that line me, the bridges that cross me,
everything, louder and louder,
faster as I roll, as I tear
right into the arms, back into the belly — *nothing*
can stop me — *of my mother again.*

A STREAK OF BLOOD THAT
ONCE WAS A TINY RED SPIDER

is all there is left of it which walked
down the page of a book
and which I meant only to brush away
but crushed
to this minuscule skid mark — 4 mm high, ½ mm wide: baby
red scar, somewhat askew

hyphen forever
on page 211 of *Lost Tribes and Promised Lands*.
It had many legs — it was moving fast.
Some version of a heart must have been in there.
Some sensory talents.
Descending down a page,

little literate one, you came to the end of your page,
and thus published
I close your tomb to a sound
I love — hollow, soft: *whump,*
and give it back to a shelf
and again, someday, I hope, a reader.

EMILY'S MOM

(Emily Norcross Dickinson, 1804–1882,
mother of Emily Elizabeth Dickinson, 1830–1886)

Today we'd say she was depressed, clinically. Then,
they called it "nameless disabling apathy," "persistent nameless
infirmity," "often she fell sick
with nameless illnesses and wept
with quiet resignation." *The Nameless,* they should
have called it! She was *depressed,*
unhappy, and who can blame her
given her husband, Edward, who was, without exception,
absent — literally and otherwise — and in comparison
to a glacial range, cooler by a few degrees.
Febrile, passionate: not Edward.
"From the first she was desolately lonely."
A son gets born, a daughter (the poet), another daughter,
and that's all, then nearly fifty years
of "tearful withdrawal and obscure maladies."
She was depressed, for christsake! The Black Dog
got her, the Cemetery Sledge, the Airless Vault,
it ate her up
and her options few: no Prozac then, no Elavil,
couldn't eat *all* the rum cake,
divorce the sluggard?
Her children? Certainly they
brought her some joy?: "I always ran home to Awe
when a child, if anything befell me. He was an Awful Mother,
but I liked him better than none."
This is what her daughter, the poet, said.
No, it had her,
for a good part of a century
it had her by the neck: the Gray Python,
the Vortex Vacuum.
During the last long (seven) years,
crippled further by a stroke,
it did not let go but, *but*: "We were never intimate
Mother and children while she was our Mother

but mines in the ground meet by tunneling
and when she became our Child, the Affection came."
This is what Emily, her daughter, wrote
in that manner wholly hers,
the final word
on Emily, her mother — melancholic,
fearful, starved-of-love.

"MR JOHN KEATS FIVE FEET TALL"
SAILS AWAY

on the *Maria Crowther,*
a cargo brig
of 127 tons bound for Italy,
Naples, the sun
which was thought would cure his cough, his lungs.
The day: Sunday, 17 September 1820.
With him: Severn,
a painter, his nurse-companion;
Mrs. Pidgeon, a pain in the ass
and cold; Miss Cotterell,
like Keats consumptive
and "very lady-like but a sad martyr
to her illness," wrote Severn;
the captain and crew.
This was not a pleasure cruise.
Second day out: the sick
and nonsick get seasick
and "bequeath to the mighty sea their breakfasts."
Storms, water by the pailful
in the sleeping cabin; calms, nary a puff.
A squall (Bay of Biscay),
a calm again (Cape Saint Vincent),
then, one dawn, Gibraltar, the African coast!
Then, Bay of Naples,
Saturday, 21 October — ten days
quarantined
during which not one porthole opened
it rained so hard and long.
Welcome, Mr. Keats, to sunny southern Italy.
Then, by wagon, on roads ripe
with malaria, to Rome
from where in the two months plus
he still has lungs
he does not write again to Fanny Brawne,
whom he loves,

though he does write about
her to a friend
the famous sentence: "Oh God! God! God!" (in whom
he had no faith) "Every thing
I have in my trunk
reminds me of her
and goes through me like a spear."
And the better but less quoted
next sentence: "The silk
lining she put in my travelling cap scalds
my head." The verb choice "scalds"
perfect here (literally he had the fever,
figuratively . . .), the tactility
fresher, the melodrama cut
by an almost comic hyperbole. It is
more Keats than Keats,
who died 172 years, 8 months, 2 weeks, and 4 days
ago — this tiny man
John Keats,
who wrote some poems
without which,
inch by inch — in broken
barn light,
in classrooms (even there!),
under the lamp where what you read
teaches you what you love — without which
we would each,
inch by hammered inch,
we would each
be diminished.

A man risked his life to write the words.
A man hung upside down (an idiot friend
holding his legs?) with spray paint
to write the words on a girder fifty feet above
a highway. And his beloved,
the next morning driving to work . . . ?
His words are not (meant to be) so unique.
Does she recognize his handwriting?
Did he hint to her at her doorstep the night before
of "something special, darling, tomorrow"?
And did he call her at work
expecting her to faint with delight
at his celebration of her, his passion, his risk?
She will *know* I love her now,
the *world* will know my love for her!
A man risked his life to write the words.
Love is like this at the bone, we hope, love
is like this, Sweatheart, all sore and dumb
and dangerous, ignited, blessed — always,
regardless, no exceptions,
always in blazing matters like these: blessed.

SAY YES

— *Rachel*

The soul of each silkworm who gave each thread
of silk sings
your blouse

in the other world knowing
it touched you, your — say yes — arms, breasts;
and the wind, between your shoulders,

unsuccessful at being cold,
and the blue water
you lift to your face, each micro-

organism in it
stunned: if consciousness
were assigned,

then these things
would be delirious
desiring — say yes — to touch

any part of you, and glad, a fire-fed-
with-solid-oxygen glad — say yes — to be, in turn,
touched by you.

GLOW WORM

We are all worms but I am a glow worm.
— Winston Churchill

Lost in self, drowned; asphyxiated in ego,
blind to same: the dog-
after-a-gut-wagon drivenness, self-righteousness,
all (*the male is small, winged, the female*

larger, wingless) to fill
the memory hole
with matter or to extract
from the final bone its marrow.

In spite, the glow worm's inner fire
is chemical, cold, cold,
and therefore false
in drawing others to it for love.

The word sounds like the thing.
The sound of the word next to
the sound of another word
sounds like the thing feels
or you desire it to feel. You want
this alive
from its insides
and the mind, the denotative, the dictionary
means naught: what you want
to be known must be known
cellularly, belly-wise,
or on the tongue: *cerulean blue,*
for example, or *punch drunk.*
Those who live elsewhere
than their bodies don't buy it, don't like it,
this in-the-body; the science
and the math tests on it
are yet inconclusive.
There's always this little humming
beneath the surface
of the painting, the dance, the play
(the good ones) that tells your heart
that it — the painting, the dance, the play — tells
a truth: *dewlap, dewlap,*
it's dawn's time, it says — the sound
provides the thing its lungs, mouth,
and blood-beat. The sound, the noise of the sound, is
the thing — the deaf can hear it,
the blind see it, this tuning fork
beneath the breastbone, sweetly
accompanying its song.

Sixty miles from a lake,
no river or pond within forty-eight,
no ocean near,
and this rowboat, crisply painted, oarlocks
oiled, oars set and cocked,
in a small — mossy, pine needles — clearing
of sparse gray and yellow forest grass.
The light here: like joy, pain, like glass.
On its bow, in red paint, beside the anchor rope,
its name: *A Joy To Be Hidden*
But a Disaster Not To Be Found.
An odd place, a long name, for a boat.

Notes from *THE DROWNED RIVER*

"Traveling Exhibit of Torture Instruments": The quotes are from the exhibition catalogue Torture Instruments from the Middle Ages to the Industrial Era.

"Mr. Pope": The quotes come from, and the poem owes a lot to, Maynard Mack's biography of Alexander Pope.

"The Creature Has a Purpose": The title is a phrase of Keats's.

"At Least Let Me Explain": The quote is from Tocqueville.

Notes from *SPLIT HORIZON*

"Emily's Mom" owes a great deal to Cynthia Griffin Wolff's biography Emily Dickinson.

"'Mr John Keats Five Feet Tall' Sails Away": The quoted words in the title are Keats's own.

The italicized line in "A Boat in the Forest" is by Emily Dickinson.